DRESSING the NAKED HAND

THE WORLD'S GREATEST GUIDE TO MAKING, STAGING, AND PERFORMING WITH PUPPETS

BY AMY WHITE, MARK H. PULHAM & DALLIN BLANKENSHIP

IT'S OFFICIALLY BEGINNING! POUR THE CHAMPAGNE! CALL THE PRESS! TELL THE U.N.! TELL MY *MOM!* WE'RE FAMOOOOUUUUS!

THIS IS GOING TO BE A LONG BOOK.

YOU HAVE BEEN WARNED.

Text and Photo Copyright © 2015 by Amy White, Mark H. Pulham, and Dallin Blankenship.
Video Copyright © 2015 by Paul D. Green and PDG Productions.
Illustrations (pp. 8, 132–135) Copyright © 2015 Jess Smart Smiley.
Background photos, toolbox items, and other visuals from Shutterstock.com.

All rights reserved.

Published by Familius LLC, www.familius.com

Familius books are available at special discounts for bulk purchases for sales promotions or for family or corporate use. Special editions, including personalized covers, excerpts of existing books, or books with corporate logos, can be created in large quantities for special needs. For more information, contact Premium Sales at 559-876-2170 or email specialmarkets@familius.com.

Library of Congress Catalog-in-Publication Data

2015935374   ISBN 978-1-938301-13-1

Edited by Brooke Jorden
Cover and book design by David Miles

10 9 8 7 6 5 4 3 2 1

First Edition
2015

FAMILIUS

CONTENTS

VIDEO TUTORIAL INCLUDED ON THE DVD

DON'T MISS THE VIDEOS!

We've done our best to create easy-to-follow instructions, but nothing compares with actually watching a puppeteer at work. Fortunately, we've included video tutorials for most of the puppets and acting tips in this book. You'll find them on the DVD located in the back of the book. Trust us—they'll save you a lot of time and frustration, and we promise they'll make you laugh or your money back! (What's that? Oh. Our publisher says we can't technically promise that. Bah humbug.)

A LETTER TO THE READER: A CALL TO GREATNESS

An open book begins the journey of a thousand lives.

Allow yourself to move beyond mere trial and error. Learn from the mistakes and frustrations of uneducated self-learners. Gain access to the experienced puppet creators' minds that are found within these pages, for now is the time to explore your inner puppet like you've never been able to before.

Unleash the characters that reside within your soul, the voiceless, as-yet-unrealized alter egos that await the opportunity to be clothed by their creator's hand. Today is the day to take upon yourself the puppeteer's challenge and give life to previously hidden talent.

Beware the naysayers, those who believe that the puppet will one day rule the world and that revealing the mysteries of the puppet is to pave the way to an eventual takeover. Such radicalization is a myth, a rumor blown out of proportion. It is through mutual understanding that humankind and puppetkind will find room to grow in harmonious, er . . . harmony.

It is not an easy path the puppeteer takes. As with any creative endeavor, there will be challenges. The wise artist will remember that any perceived creative mistake is, in truth, opportunity cloaked in disguise. With dedication and a good dose of determination, the day will come when you will find yourself living the life of one who is never alone, one who carries with them a bountiful bevy of puppet friends and a newly felted and furred family.

Remember: you too can be one of the fabled few, a notable noble, the greatest of greats—a puppeteer.

In the end, you should ask yourself: *What is a puppet, if not a dressing for the naked hand?* One does not exist without the other. And if you find—even if it's to your imminent surprise—that puppetry is more than a passing fancy and has become a full-fledged passion, we promise to welcome you, with open arms, into this brave new world.

Yours sincerely,
Amy White, Mark Pulham, and Dallin Blankenship

LONG LIVE THE REVERED PARTNERSHIP THAT IS PUPPET AND PUPPETEER

A
HISTORY
LESSON

IN THE BEGINNING . . .

The legend of puppetry and the art of the puppet share a long and complex history with humankind.

Rising from the shadows, the legends have grown. Beginning with mere hand shapes—shadows thrown into relief against firelit walls—puppets then emerged in stick, clay, and woven fabrications and finally grew to include the papier-mâché, foam, felt, rubber, wood, and glue masterpieces found in nearly every culture. This ancient form of animating stories continues to capture imaginations the world over.

This is the story of the puppet.

SHADOW PUPPETS

In the beginning, there was shadow, and there was light. And it came to pass that the shadow was separated from the light . . . the light of the evening fire. And early man discovered he could tell stories against illuminated cavern walls. And in that light, the first puppets were created, and they were called good, and man named them "Hand Shadows."

WAYANG PUPPETS

In the following years, the great Shadow Puppets of Indonesia were created. It is here that we find the harmonious partnership of human, *Dalang*, and puppet, *Wayang* (Japanese for "shadow"), also known as *Gamelan* in Java or the *Bayangan* of Bali or Malay.

Working together, puppets and humans created wondrous performances of light and shadow. These tales of romance, along with classic Indonesian stories, were often told alongside an accompanying orchestra for many a special or royal occasion.

Traditionally crafted of buffalo hide and mounted on bamboo sticks, these magnificent constructions are now known as "shadow rod puppets."

PARADE DRAGON PUPPETS

In the Far East, enormous parade puppets—Chinese dragons, emblems of guardianship and vigilance—were created. These giants of the puppet world were designed to be carried by as many as fifty people. A wondrous sight, this fearsome lot was oft considered a harbinger of good luck.

With the help of a human gymnast who, leaping and dancing, controls the dragon's head, this undulating puppet follows the lead of the "precious pearl," a ball carried atop a long pole.

Often constructed of bamboo hoops and covered with rich fabrics, these puppet dragons may stretch up to one hundred feet in length.

MARIONETTE PUPPETS

Traveling to France, we find the masterful carvers of the marionette. Named for the popular religious character Mary—the word marionette literally means "little Mary" in French—these nimble actors are another example of the beautiful partnership of human and puppet.

Operated via strings and wires suspended from a handheld controller, these hinged puppets were allowed unmatched freedom compared to other puppets. This type of puppet manipulation demands great skill on the part of the marionettist (yes, I think I made that up) or puppeteer.

In Burma, these suspension puppets were often used to teach manners, to bear messages, and even to carry not-so-subtle reprimands from frustrated rulers to their people. Meanwhile, in Greece and Rome, these stringed artisans could be found performing the great works of Aristotle.

And yet, despite the use of marionettes in all parts of the world—including the ancient North American Hopi tribe—some claim that Italy is the true birthplace of the illustrious marionette. It is from these roots that the itinerant troublemaker Pinocchio, of the Tells-No-Lies Clan, claims his heritage.

GLOVE PUPPETS

Idling about old Italy, one would have found Mister Punch, formerly known as Punchinello—a trickster and a lord of misrule—and his wife, Judy, or, as she was originally called, Joan.

These two glove puppets, Punch and Judy, along with their companions—Baby, Constable, Joey the Clown, Crocodile, Monkey, Skeleton, and Doctor, among others—arrived in England in the 1600s amid the cheers and jeers of their mostly adult audiences. The puppeteer, also known as the Professor, was assisted by the Bottler, a human who would corral the audience for the show.

The story of Punch and Judy spans centuries, one wherein they became a traditional favorite that played to kings and queens, presidents and paupers, and even, it is said, the great Shakespeare.

BUNRAKU PUPPETS

Bunraku (which has nothing to do with bunnies or haikus) is yet another of the puppet greats, and if you really wanted, you could write a haiku in tribute to the grand Japanese Bunraku puppets, maybe something involving bunnies and random acts of the kind sort. Quite literally, *bunraku* means "puppets and storytelling."

Typically two to four feet tall, the head of the Bunraku are traditionally carved by sophisticated specialists, while their bodies are created by puppeteers. Bunraku are manipulated by a highly trained trio of humans. The master controller operates the head and right arm, the left puppeteer controls the left arm, and the third puppeteer maneuvers the feet and legs. Hidden by their black clothing, these craftsmen can spend up to thirty years in training.

The Bunraku are another successful example of puppet and human harmony.

MOUTH PUPPETS

In the latter part of the twentieth century, puppets evolved from the easily manipulated mouth puppets—such as those found on the famed *Kukla, Fran, and Ollie Show*—into the celebrated (and distinctly styled) Jim Henson puppets. This new breed of head, hand, and rod puppets is a successful and beloved story, one that is still being played out today . . .

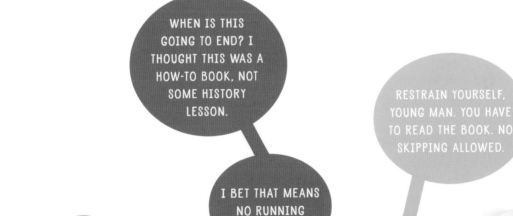

PART I

CREATING THE MASTERPIECE

PUPPET-MAKING WORKSHOPS, FROM BEGINNING TO ADVANCED

(SIGH)

JUST GREAT, I *HATE* MUSHY SCENES.

chapter 1

STUFFET PUPPET WORKSHOP

THE MAKING OF A SIMPLE STUFFED PUPPET

FOLLOW ALONG WITH MARK IN "WHIPPING UP WONDERS"

STUFFET PUPPET PREP

On your mark, get set, and let's go! Scavenge up a variety of those stuffy old animals—new ones or second-chancers from the thrift stores—or go digging down deep in your closets. Most prospective puppeteers will have something stashed away in there, no matter how old they are.

wash before you wear

First things first. If your future puppet was a formerly owned stuffed animal, you might consider giving it a good wash.

1 Package the prospective puppet in a protective pillowcase before you begin the wash, thus protecting both your puppet and your washing machine.

2 Use the gentle cycle with warm water, adding a good dose of fabric softener—the really good-smelling kind. Spin on high.

3 Do not dry with heat: it melts eyes, corkscrews whiskers, and fizzles fur. Instead, a nice tumble on the air-dry setting is recommended.

SPEED DRY

In a hurry? Short on time? If you are opening your animal up immediately, you can remove the stuffing for a quick fluff and dry outside the confines of the puppet.

ANOTHER DRYING METHOD

Or you can place the animal in front of a fan for a few days. Rotate it like a rotisserie chicken every so often.

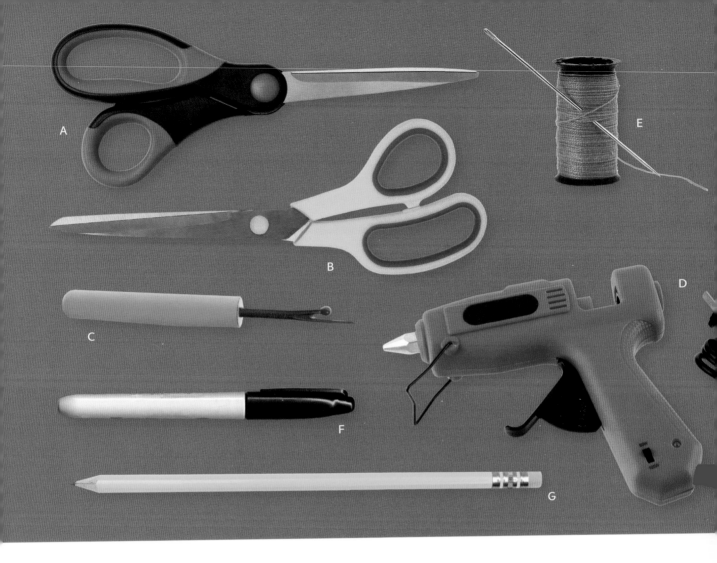

Once your animals have been sufficiently counseled and prepared, you only need a few easy-to-locate tools and supplies to finalize your Stuffet puppet creations.

stuffet tool kit supplies

A Scissors—the nobody-better-be-touching-my-good-scissors pair

B Scissors—the crafting pair that isn't so good

C Seam ripper (optional)

D Hot glue gun and glue sticks

E Needle and heavy-duty thread

F Permanent marker

G Pencil

Got it all gathered? Now, all it takes are a few nips and tucks before you will be bringing these refreshed and ready animals out of retirement and into the exciting world of puppetry.

POLYSTYRENE? KEEP MR. SHOP-VAC CLOSE AT HAND

Stay away from polystyrene foam-stuffed animals. If you don't believe me, or you absolutely have to rescue a willing Stuffet, you can attempt it. Make sure the vacuum is close by; or better yet, haul in that wet/dry vac from the garage. You are going to need it. Oh, and make sure the setting is set for vac'ing (in); no shopping (out) allowed.

STUFFET FINGER PUPPET MINI

2–3

1

4

These finger-sized little guys are perfect for carrying along in a purse or tote for easy and instant entertainment opportunities. They are great tantrum stoppers, too.

supplies

- Stuffet Tool Kit
- Stuffed animal, small
- Sock, small—very small

The hardest part is taking that first cut—not unlike ripping off a bandage. Gird your loins, gather your courage, and just do it.

directions

1 Assess the best location (usually the bottom or lower back of the stuffed animal) and cut a finger-sized opening along a seam with a seam ripper; or if there is no seam, carefully cut an opening with a pair of sharp scissors.

2 Remove enough stuffing so that you can comfortably fit the sock and your finger inside.

3 Stuff the sock into the cavity you've created in the puppet. If the sock is too big and the end of the sock sticks out of the puppet opening, you will want to trim it by cutting off the excess.

4 Whipstitch or hot glue the sock to the opening of the Finger Stuffet to finish.

VARIATIONS

slip-proof puppets

Instead of a small sock, use the fingertip of a rubber glove and hot glue it in. Turn the glove inside out for better traction. The rubbery surface helps prevent accidental mid-story loss of puppet.

THREE'S A CROWD

Use a glove instead of a sock to create a family or cast of characters. It's a great way to liven up the old bedtime routine and bring your stories to life. Remember: the family that plays together, stays together.

1-2

3-4

ISN'T HE CUTE?

STUFFET HEAD CUDDLY
(head movement only)

ladybug example

You can't go wrong with a Cuddly. This little character loves to tuck his head in for a good snuggle and is more than willing to be there for you when you have a hankering for a little bit of quiet time.

supplies

- Stuffet Tool Kit
- Stuffed animal, about hand size
- Sock, medium size

directions

1 Find the seam in the back of the stuffed animal and open up a hole big enough for your hand to slip inside.

2 Remove enough stuffing so that your sock-encased hand will fit nicely inside with your fingers reaching up into the head or nose area.

3 Stick your sock-covered hand into the opening, then remove your hand, leaving the sock inside.

4 Trim the excess sock, if necessary, by cutting off any portion that doesn't fit inside the puppet.

5 Stretch the opening as wide as possible and hand stitch or hot glue the neck of the sock to the puppet opening.

1–2

3–4

KEEP IT FROM POPPING!

Sew or glue the seams at maximum stretch to prevent seams from popping later if they are accidentally overstretched.

(COUGH) CHARMING.

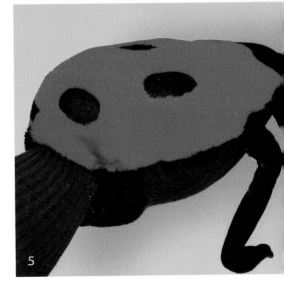

5

GET AN OVERVIEW
IN "WHIPPING UP
WONDERS" VIDEO #4

STUFFET ARM AND LEG WRIGGLY
(moveable arms and legs)

With waving arms and optional wriggly legs, these glove-like and friendly Stuffets make ideal huggable companions.

supplies

- Stuffet Tool Kit
- Stuffed animal, one that will comfortably fit on your hand
- Glove, of the stretchy variety

FLOPPY ARM FIX

Shorten a too-long, too-floppy arm by cutting out the middle (elbow or wrist segment) as much as is needed or desired and then sewing the hand back on.

directions

1 Open up the back seam of the puppet with the seam ripper, or cut it open with a pair of scissors. Make the hole big enough to allow your hand to fit comfortably inside with the opening at your wrist.

2 Remove enough stuffing so that your gloved hand fits inside the animal's arms, legs, and head with your fingers spread apart. After putting on the glove, stick your thumb and pinky in the legs, your ring and pointer fingers in the arms, and your middle finger in the nose or head.

3 Once positioned, remove your hand, leaving the glove in place, and stretch the opening as wide as possible. Hand stitch or hot glue the base of the glove into the opening.

4 If you are feeling adventurous, you can add a few more stitches in the ends of the glove fingers to keep the glove in place. This is best done with one hand inside—stretching the glove—for better placement. Better yet, get a willing (and thick-skinned) volunteer—preferably not siblings who are currently in contretemps with each other.

WHAT SIZE STUFFED ANIMAL?

A Wriggly candidate will fit like a big glove on your hand, like these.

FOLLOW ALONG
IN "WHIPPING UP
WONDERS" VIDEO #1

STUFFET TALKIE

Not satisfied with the occasional snuggle and cuddle? With just a few additional supplies, you can get the conversation started with a wide-mouthed Stuffet Talking Puppet.

SAY "AAAH." WHAT? YOU DON'T HAVE A TONGUE? WE CAN FIX THAT.

SURE, WE CAN GIVE HIM *YOURS*.

SUGGESTED MOUTHPIECE MATERIALS:

Foam cores, cereal boxes, file folders, mouse pads, plastic placemats, or sheets of craft foam are all great mouthpiece options. The coating on the outside of cereal boxes acts as a moisture barrier, and the hinge fold is already there for you. You can even glue together a few layers for thickness and durability. Additionally, book board is firm yet manageable. Craft foam and foam core poster boards are convenient and easy.

supplies

- Stuffet Tool Kit
- Stuffed animal
- Fleece or felt
- Heavy poster board, cuttable plastic, or other mouthpiece materials (see Suggested Mouthpiece Materials on opposite page)
- Adhesive (contact cement, spray adhesive, tacky glue, white glue, or PVA glue)
- Gaffer's tape (or other fabric-backed tape with heat-resistant adhesive)
- Long-legged sock, preferably of the single variety (Got a hole in the toe? No problem.)

directions

1 Open up your prospective Talkie—be it from the back, from the head, or from underneath—by following a seam and using seam rippers, or cut an opening with sharp scissors.

2 Feel around inside the stuffed animal for any tied down threads or hidden seams that sometimes lurk in these larger stuffed animals. Often you can either cut through or open up the seams with a few judicious snips of the scissors. Feel around in the mouth area and plan the best size and location for a mouth.

3 If your stuffed animal already has a mouth that opens and shuts and does not require a mouth to be cut into it:

- You can stop here and move on to sewing or gluing the sock in the back opening in the same manner as found in the previous Stuffet sections.
- If you would like to firm up or reinforce the mouth, continue into the Making the Stuffet Mouthpiece section, skipping Step 1.

4 If your stuffed animal does not have a mouth that will open and shut and needs to have a mouth cut into it, move on to the "Making the Stuffet Mouthpiece" section.

LESS STUFFING IS MORE

Consider removing some of the stuffing before you close the puppet up. Less is usually more, and a loosely stuffed puppet leaves lots of room for not only the hand but also plenty of hugs. Note that it takes four hugs a day to survive, eight to be healthy, and twelve for true wellness and growth. I read that online, so it must be true.

FOLLOW ALONG
IN "WHIPPING UP
WONDERS" VIDEO #2

MAKING THE STUFFET MOUTHPIECE

If your stuffed animal does not already have a mouth that will open and shut, you will need to cut open the mouth area on the puppet.

directions

1 Using the puppet you have prepared in the Stuffet Talkie section, carefully, and with great consideration, cut a mouth-wide opening. Test the opening with your hand. Does it feel wide enough? Is there room to move your fingers?

2 After selecting your preferred mouthpiece material, fold it in half and place the fold inside the mouth of the puppet as if the puppet were biting the piece.

3 Trace around the puppet's bite with a marker on the top and bottom jaws. If you are working with a lighter-colored puppet, be careful not to get ink on the fur.

4 Cut out the traced mouthpiece shape. Cut larger than your traced lines, test the fit, and trim as needed. Test the fit of the mouthpiece inside the puppet mouth. Trim again if necessary.

5 Glue a piece of felt onto one side (what will become the visible side of the mouth) of the mouthpiece using glue or adhesive. One of our go-to favorites is spray adhesive. If your puppet did not require cutting a mouth opening, the felt is optional, and you can move on to Step 8.

6 When the glue or adhesive is dry, trim the felt down to size, leaving a 1/4-inch to 1/2-inch border of felt around the mouthpiece material.

7 Test the shape in the puppet's mouth again.

8 Now comes the tricky part. Cut the toe of the sock to open it up across the seam of the toe area. Test the size of the hole against the circumference of the mouthpiece as you go. It should look like the sock is swallowing the mouthpiece.

9 CAREFULLY hot glue the edge of the sock onto the non-felted side (or either side, if you skipped the felt step) of the mouthpiece. When you are done, you will have a snake-ish mouth tunnel.

DON'T GET BURNED

If you roll the cut edge of the sock under a bit, it gives an extra layer of protection between your fingers and the hot glue.

Also, if you dip your fingertips in water before working with hot glue, the glue is less likely to stick to your skin. Warning: hot glue is hot. Very, very hot.

AND DON'T LICK YOUR FINGERS! JUST USE A CUP OF WATER.

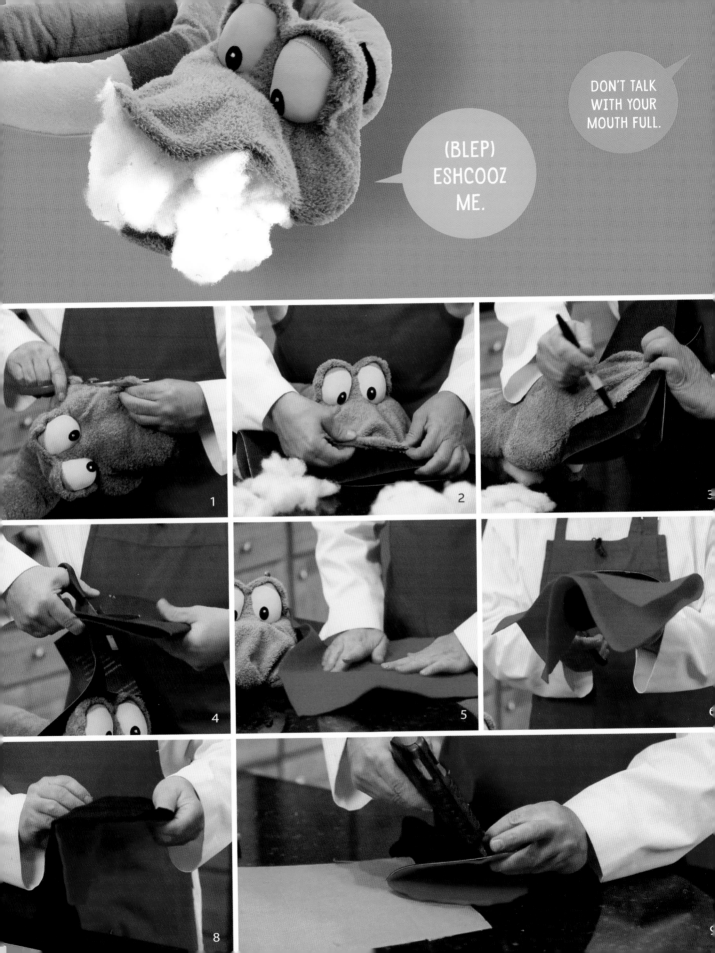

PLACING THE STUFFET MOUTHPIECE

option 1: stuffed animal with pre-existing mouth

If your animal already has a mouth that opens and closes, all you are doing is reinforcing it to make it puppeteer friendly. You will just need to carefully glue the mouthpiece into the mouth of the puppet.

1 Insert your hand and arm into the sock, all the way to the mouth. Insert your sock-encased arm into the puppet. Test the fit and placement. Once satisfied, remove the mouthpiece and move on to Step 2.

2 Spread or spray adhesive onto the portion of the mouthpiece that will become the inside (the invisible side glued onto the inside of the puppet's existing mouth fabric) of the mouth and carefully insert your sock-encased hand and arm into the puppet.

3 When positioned correctly, pinch the existing mouth closed and hold it until the glue is dry enough to keep the mouthpiece in place. Run your fingers around all the edges to affirm good adhesion. If possible, you can turn the puppet inside out for this step.

4 After gluing the mouthpiece into the puppet, make sure the puppet is right side out again, and skip to Step 9 of Option 2.

option 2: stuffed animal without pre-existing mouth

FOLLOW ALONG IN "WHIPPING UP WONDERS" VIDEO #3

If your animal needed to have the mouth cut open, gluing a mouthpiece into a once-closed animal's mouth is best achieved with a hot glue gun.

1 Insert your hand and arm into the sock, all the way to the prepared mouthpiece. Insert your sock-encased arm into the puppet. Test the fit of the mouth.

2 Align the center of both the puppet fabric and the puppet mouthpiece—top jaw, then bottom jaw. Hot glue the center of the fabric to the center of the mouthpiece.

3 Mark the middle of the front edge of both the mouthpiece and the puppet's jaws, right between where the two front teeth would normally reside (that's four marks in total: two center marks on the mouthpiece and two on the puppet's fabric) where the marks won't bleed through or be seen, please.

4 Align your marks and, starting with either the top jaw or the lower jaw, run a thin, short line of hot glue over the marking on the mouthpiece.

FUME WARNING

Be careful of spray adhesive overspray. Seriously. If you want to keep your puppet-building rights and your familial relationships intact, consider doing this step outside—not to mention the ever-smart avoidance of harmful fumes that will accumulate if done indoors. And for safety's sake, follow all manufacturer cautions.

TOO MUCH GLUE!

If you do accidentally use too much glue, and it oozes out onto the felt of the mouth, spread some fur over the still-hot glue to hide the mistake. If your puppet is not so hairy, consider adding teeth later.

5 Roll the fabric of the animal's lip up and onto the glue. Be careful of squishing the hot glue out and into a place that will be visible.

6 Repeat Steps 4 and 5 for the other jaw.

7 Slowly, and in small segments, continue to hot glue the mouthpiece into the puppet's mouth by slightly wrapping the fur (lip) of the puppet over and onto the inside edge of the felted side of the mouthpiece. Be sure to cover any view of the sock, for both aesthetics and durability.

8 Work from the center to the corners of the mouth. If the mouth opening is bigger than the mouthpiece, close it up by hand stitching it closed and then gluing the newly stitched corner of the mouth to the mouthpiece.

9 Trim the sock, if needed, and either whipstitch or hot glue the sock to the puppet's opened back to finish off the puppet.

variation

Do you have an animal that really wants to talk but the poor baby is a bit on the smaller side of things? If you can fit a finger in the lower jaw, you can get it talking. Use the fingertip of a stretchy glove in lieu of a sock. Don't worry about a mouthpiece, either; just do a modified version of the Cuddly, going in through the back of the neck or head, and just use one, two, or three fingers (in a pull-down motion) to manipulate the mini-mouthed Talkie.

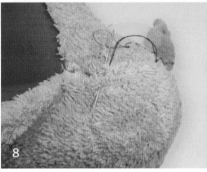

HAIRY LIPS

Hot glue and puppet fur do not coexist in a friendly manner. Extreme care must be taken so that your puppet doesn't end up with a cankerous growth of glue muck instead of the much-preferred and visually appealing hairy lip.

STUFFED ANIMAL WITH PRE-EXISTING MOUTH, REINFORCED USING OPTION 1

STUFFED ANIMAL WITHOUT PRE-EXISTING MOUTH, CREATED USING OPTION 2

chapter 2

HAND PUPPET LABORATORY

POPULATING A PLANET OF PUPPET PEOPLES

FOLLOW ALONG WITH MARK IN

"FRANKENPUPPET"

PUPPET-PEOPLE PREP

Ready to take the next step in puppet making? Be it bird, monster, human, or animal, the wide-mouthed Hand Puppet is a perfect blank canvas to work with in this next level of puppet creation.

Start with what you know. Take a good long look in the mirror and let's see about making a miniature-sized you. Gather your tools and add a few easy-to-collect supplies, and you will be off to a fabulous start. In this section, each step has several possible options. Be sure to choose which options you prefer before you begin so you can be sure to have all the necessary materials.

hand puppet tool kit

A   Scissors—the nobody-better-be-touching-my-good-scissors pair

B   Scissors—the crafting pair that isn't so good

C   Self-healing cutting mat

D   Utility knife (breakaway blade, carpet blade, and/or razor blade)

E   Hot glue gun and glue sticks

F   Permanent marker

G   Pencil

H   Sewing pins

I   Sewing machine and thread

J   Needle and quilting or heavy-duty thread

K   Wooden spoon or dowel

WARNING:

Puppets in the following section tend to take over workshops, hijack puppet makers, and, like many a toddling tyrant (or teenage trauma queen), are immune—for all intents and purposes—to most forms of persuasion.

IT'S ALIIIIIIIVE!

HOW TO MAKE A HAND PUPPET

FOLLOW ALONG IN
"FRANKENPUPPET"
VIDEO #2

MAKE IT LAST

*Vellux®, fleece, or fur makes a much more durable skin than felt or flannel. Face it: you're going to put a lot of work into your puppet; you want it to last, don't you? Consider further protection by spraying your creations with a coat of Scotchgard®. As with sunscreen, an ounce of prevention is worth a pound of cure.

SAFETY FIRST!

**Read all safety instructions carefully. Adhesives and tools can be very dangerous—from toxic fumes and ruined clothing to dangerous cuts and damaged surfaces. Know before you go, and be safe.

MAKING THE HEAD

option 1: soft and sewn

This soft-sided puppet is a delight to work with, and it's one of the easier puppets to make as it only requires a skin—no foam bones are necessary.

supplies

- Hand Puppet Tool Kit
- Fleece, Vellux®, fur, or other puppet skin* (recycle and use an old fleece coat or blanket)
- Felt
- Adhesive (contact adhesive or spray adhesive)**
- Batting
- Mouthpiece (see next section for materials and instructions)
- Soft and Sewn Head pattern (see page 149)

NOTE: If your puppet patterns are going to be heavily, or even moderately, used, consider transferring them to interfacing instead of standard paper. Non-fusible Pellon® and other stiff and non-fraying utility fabrics make for long-lasting patterns that will stand the test of many hands, many uses, and many hours of abuse. Or recycle those old file folders—you know, the good, thick kind—by tracing your patterns out on them. They won't last as long as the interfacing, but it beats filling up a landfill with something that still can be useful.

directions

1 Choose the puppet skin material. (Vellux®, fleece, etc.)

2 Determine the nap and stretch of your skin fabric.

3 Fold material in half, right sides (furry sides) together.

4 Pin pattern (see page 149) onto the material.

5 Cut material out, including the triangle-shaped darts. Depending on the type of material, choose the best cutting method:

- If cutting a low- to no-pile Vellux® or fleece, you can cut the same as you would any normal material without the special consideration that is needed for a long-pile fur.
- If cutting fur of any moderate to long length, you will want to slide the tip of the scissors under the fur itself and only cut along the base of the strands, or the mesh bond portion. This leaves the fur strands long and luxurious. See page 140 in the Resources section for more details on cutting fur.

SEWING TIP:

Adjusting for seam allowances is optional and something you can tailor to your personal tastes and hand size.

WATCH THE FUR

If the fur has a definite direction, align the pattern accordingly. An upside-down pattern will leave your puppet with, at best, upward-pointing hair, and at worst, a half-up, half-down split personality. Unless that's the look you were going for, it's best to double-check that nap. The same goes for the stretch; if you prefer that the stretch go around the girth or the height of the puppet, position the pattern in line with your needs.

CUTTING TIP

When using a low-pile or fleece material, trace the pattern, then instead of cutting the material immediately, sew around the tracing; finally, cut the sewn fabric shape around the outside edges of the material. Just make sure you don't accidentally cut through a seam; leave an adequate seam allowance.

SEWING A DART

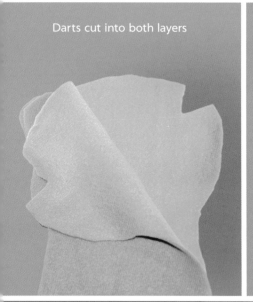

Darts cut into both layers

Dart pinned and sewn

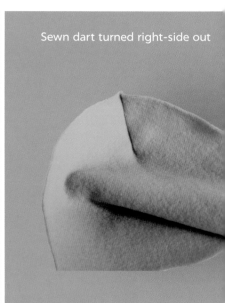

Sewn dart turned right-side out

OUCH!
REALLY? BY HAND, YOU SAY? NOT SO EASY WHEN YOU'VE ONLY GOT THREE FINGERS.

NO SEWING MACHINE?

No worries. The reverse ladder stitch and the whipstitch are excellent alternatives. Additionally, when working with medium- to long-pile furs, your seams are easier to disguise when hand stitched. See page 144 in the Resources section for different hand stitches you can try.

6 Separate the two halves of fabric. One at a time, pin the darts with the right sides together and sew. (See page 143 in the Resources section to learn about darts.)

HOW TO SEW FUR

Low-pile materials can be sewn with a machine or by hand. Consider sewing medium- to long-pile furs by hand. This method will allow you to hide the seams more effectively. If sewing furs by machine, try to move as much of the fur out from under the presser foot and into the body of the puppet as possible. This allows the seams to mesh more naturally. A soft-bristle brush is a great tool to assist you, not to mention that most puppets enjoy the extra attention.

7 Pin the two halves with the right sides together (fur on the inside). Match up the sewn dart seams, then the mouth and sides.

8 Sew the center seam from the top lip, up over the head, and to the back of the neck. Next, sew from the front of the neck up to the bottom lip. Leave the puppeteer's hand access and the mouth openings unsewn.

9 Move to the Hand Puppet Mouthpiece section on page 40 and choose from the Folded, Hinged, or Shaped Sheet Foam Mouth for your puppet.

MAKING THE HEAD

option 2: shaped sheet foam puppet

Once you get a feel for making these firm-bodied yet versatile and fun puppets, you may want to mix up the order in which you assemble them. Do what feels natural; there are no hard-and-fast rules when working on creative impulse.

supplies

- Hand Puppet Tool Kit
- Sheet of poly foam cushion, approximately 1–2 inches thick (available in most craft stores)
- Fleece, Vellux®, or your favorite skin material*
- Poly foam
- Spray adhesive
- Shaped Sheet Foam head pattern (see page 154)

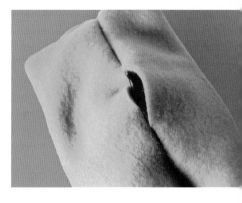

HOW TO FIX A POPPED SEAM

The wise seamstress/seamster turns the puppet right side out, tests, and then fixes any slipped or popped seams before proceeding to the mouthpiece.

To fix a popped seam, mark the location, turn the puppet inside out, and sew over the missed segment.

Stretchy Fleece

Sheet Foam

CHOOSE YOUR SKIN WISELY

*The best skins are made of soft, stretchy, forgiving, and flexible fabrics. Save the cottons, leathers, and plastics for embellishments or different projects.

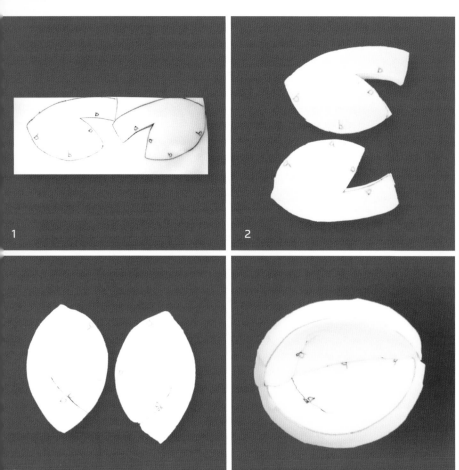

WATCH THOSE FUMES

Remember, watch that overspray. Avoid harmful fumes and distraught mothers by taking this step outside.

BEFORE YOU CUT . . .

Before cutting foam, place your project on a thick piece of cardboard or a self-healing mat to prevent unwanted carpet cutout or a permanent puppet pattern carved in your work table.

WARNING:

Foam will dull blades. Disposable- or break-away-bladed utility knives are extraordinarily useful.

directions

1 Using the Sheet Foam Puppet Head pattern on page 154, trace the pattern onto foam with a permanent marker. Label pieces and sides (A side, B side) according to the pattern labels before cutting for easier assembly later.

2 Cut all the foam pieces with a utility knife, serrated carving knife, or craft scissors. Keep blade at a 90-degree angle to the foam. It will take some practice, but it's worth the effort. A squared cut makes for smoother seams and a better puppet. When you have cut everything out, move on to Step 3.

3 Following the spray adhesive or contact adhesive instructions and safety guidelines, glue the foam pieces together as directed on the pattern. Glue the A sides (the darts) together to force each piece to curve.

4 Then, glue both pieces together along the B sides. Check that all your glue seams are holding well and spot glue as needed.

Congratulations! You now have a naked puppet skull. Move on to the Adding the Shaped Skin section, and let's get some skin on these foam bones.

adding the shaped skin

1 After choosing the puppet's skin fabric, fold the fabric in half, right sides together.

2 Pin the pattern onto the fabric. (You can use either the Soft and Sewn Head pattern on page 149 or the Simple "No Dart" Puppet pattern on page 153.)

3 Cut the pattern out of the fabric. Include the triangle-shaped darts and the mouth. Depending on the type of material, choose the best cutting method. (Refer back to page 35 for tips on cutting different materials.)

4 Separate the two halves of fabric. One at a time, pin the darts with right sides together, and sew.

Note: A sewing machine is recommended for fleece, Vellux®, or other non-hairy material. But if you've got fur, sewing by hand is by far the better method, allowing you to hide the seams more effectively. (See page 144.)

5 After the darts are sewn, pin the two halves of the fabric skin together—again, inside out. Sew the center seam from the top lip, up over the forehead, and down the back. Next, sew from the bottom lip, under the chin, and down the front.

6 Turn your puppet head right-side out and check your seams. Fix any slipped or popped seams, then test fit the dome head in the puppet. Glue extra bits of foam onto the foam dome for a firmer nose or bulgy eyes, but plan on removing the skull before adding your mouthpiece.

7 Choose a mouthpiece option for your puppet. Mouthpiece choice will be based on your personal preference, but note that a sewn Option 1 (see page 40) works well with a fleece or other low-pile skin, while a hot glued Option 2 (see page 41) might be the better choice for a long and luxuriously furry puppet.

8 While your foam dome (puppet brains) are being test fitted, you will want to sit back and finalize the look you want for your puppet. Is your creation calling for a set of nice, fat lips? A lower jutting jaw? An orthodontist's dream of an overbite? With its new brain, your puppet is likely to attempt some mind-to-mind melding contact, so don't rush things. Maybe the puppet prefers a non-protruding nothing at all.

SKIP THE BAD HAIR DAYS

Be aware of the grain of the fur or fabric with a definite nap—this is the direction in which the fur lies down. Remember: nothing is more frustrating than giving a puppet a permanent lease on bad hair days.

adding lips

Use the Shaped Sheet Foam Lips pattern on page 155. These football-shaped ovals are the puppet equivalent of lip-augmenting fillers and are to be used as desired.

1 After cutting the desired quantity of foam lip-filler ovals, spray glue the edges of the foam. As the glue becomes tacky and sticks to itself, roll the foam into a banana shape. Re-spray, mold, and roll until you have a nice-looking lip.

2 With the foam dome still in the puppet, start test fitting the lips. This particular pattern allows for a variety of lip placements—from above the mouth seam to below,

inside the skin or outside. Much of the lip placement will depend not only on the mouthpiece option you choose, but also on your choice in skin fabric. Variations are at times challenging but can be well worth the effort. The key is to have some fun. You might give that puppet some soft and fleecy protrusionary lips of excellent proportions. Or if the skin is a bit more inflexible, both you and your puppet might do best sticking with a stiff upper lip. Get creative with spray painted, airbrushed, fabric-covered, or just plain unaltered naked foam lips. Or go all out and experiment with alternate materials outside of the standard foam and fabric options. Don't let the sky be your limit. Push on, ever upward and onward, my illustrious and imaginative friends.

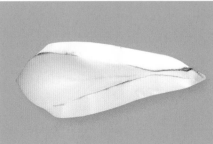

MAKING THE MOUTH

FOLLOW ALONG IN "FRANKENPUPPET" VIDEO #3

THIS MOUTH IS CLOSED

The following mouthpiece examples are closed when at rest. Mouths that are open when at rest will follow in the "Advanced Puppet-Making Workshop" section on page 77.

option 1: folded hand puppet mouthpiece

This mouthpiece works best for puppets that do not have a mouth sewn in already.

supplies

- Hand Puppet Tool Kit
- Cereal box (heavy file folders work well, too)
- Good adhesive (tacky glue, white glue, contact cement, or spray glue—again, follow all manufacturer cautions)
- Fleece or felt in desired mouth color (flesh, red, pink, black, etc.)
- Mouth pattern on page 153

directions

1 Open up and cut down the cereal box by cutting off the flaps; leave the sides connected.

2 Using one of the folds, place the box piece fold side in into the puppet's mouth.

3 Trace the puppet's bite onto the box with a permanent marker or pen.

4 Cut the cardboard mouthpiece following the traced puppet bite line.

5 Glue the cereal box to felt or fleece, leaving a 3/4-inch to 1-inch non-glued perimeter around the edge. This glue-free zone prevents gummed-up sewing needles.

6 Trim felt, using the cereal box cutout as your guide. Leave about 1/4 inch excess felt around the perimeter.

7 Fold the mouthpiece felt side in, and fit it into the inside-out puppet's mouth. At this point, every part of the puppet will be turned inside out. Test fit the mouth. Trim sparingly, if necessary.

8 With the cereal box on the bottom, carefully fit the puppet mouthpiece into the puppet's mouth opening and sew the mouthpiece into the mouth opening. Most sewing machines will sew through felt, fabric, and cereal box without a problem, and if you followed the instructions closely when gluing the felt, the sewing needle should move freely and shouldn't stick.

9 Check for popped or too-closely-sewn mouth seams, and re-sew if necessary. (See page 37.)

10 Turn puppet right side out, folding the mouthpiece back on itself as you go.

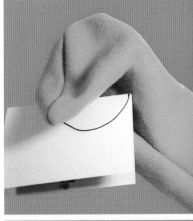

option 2: hinged hand puppet mouthpiece

This mouthpiece is best for puppets who already have a fabric mouth that needs some firming up. It will also work for a furry puppet who needs a hot-glued mouth instead of a sewn mouth.

supplies

- Hand Puppet Tool Kit
- Heavy plastic that can be cut with scissors
- Strong adhesive tape*
- Foam-adhering adhesive (contact cement or spray glue—again, follow all manufacturer cautions)
- Hot glue sticks and glue gun
- Fleece or felt (flesh, red, pink, black, etc.)

IMPROVISE

Don't have everything on the supply list? Get creative! Almost any mildly heavy plastic or thick paper such as cereal boxes or file folders that can still be cut with scissors will work; recycled plastic placemats, gallon-sized ice cream lids, ABS plastic, or even mouse pads are all usable mouthpiece materials. If it's durable and you can cut it, it's fair game.

A NOTE ON TAPE

*Most any heavy-duty tape will get the job done, but the dry adhesive found in gaffer's or binder's tape will hold out longer when put up against hot, sweaty fingers.

1–3

4

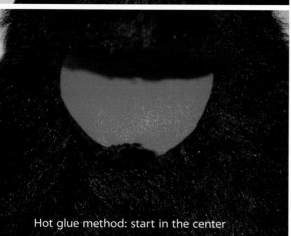

Hot glue method: start in the center

Continue gluing from the center out

I CAN TALK!

BEWARE:

Once puppets start to talk, they never, ever, ever, ever, ever, ever stop. You have been warned.

1 Choose your mouthpiece material (mouse pad, plastic, or paper product of your choice).

2 Fold the mouthpiece material in half.

3 Slide the folded portion into the puppet's open mouth. Trace the puppet's upper jaw and then lower jaw onto the mouthpiece material with a permanent marker. If the material doesn't fold well, trace top and bottom jaws separately.

4 Cut a mouthpiece, following the traced puppet bite. Test fit the piece in the puppet's mouth and trim as needed.

5 Cut the mouthpiece in half along the fold.

6 Leaving a 1/4-inch gap between the two pieces, tape both sides of the hinge. Press tape down thoroughly on both sides. Test fit the mouthpiece in the puppet.

7 Glue felt or fleece to one side of the mouthpiece material. If the mouthpiece itself will be visible to the audience, the felt will go on the soon-to-be-visible side of the mouthpiece. If the mouthpiece is meant to strengthen a fabric mouth, the felt is not really necessary.

8 Trim felt, using the mouthpiece material as your guide. Leave about a 1/4 inch of excess felt around the perimeter.

9 Turn the puppet and the newly felted mouthpiece right side out.

10 Fold the mouthpiece felt side in and fit it into the now right-side-out puppet's mouth. Test fit the mouth. Check that the puppet's fabric fits nearly perfectly around the perimeter of the mouthpiece. Trim sparingly, if necessary. Remake the mouthpiece, if needed. It will save a lot of heartache later—better a second mouthpiece than a ruined puppet.

TIP:

Spray adhesives or contact cement work well on plastic surfaces and don't bleed through or leave lumps like hot glue from a glue gun.

(SIGH) ANOTHER ONE. IS THERE NO REST FOR THE WEARY?

adhesive method for firming up a fabric mouth

- Turn the puppet inside out. Coat the side of the mouthpiece that will touch the puppet's mouth fabric with adhesive. Quickly and carefully glue the mouthpiece onto the puppet's mouth fabric. Hot glue is not recommended as an adhesive for this particular method, as it tends to form lumps and lines that are almost impossible to hide once the glue has hardened.
- When done, carefully turn the puppet right side out, using your grip on the mouthpiece as a handle. This firm grip allows you to manipulate and pull without popping the newly glued mouthpiece out like a badly fitting set of dentures.

hot glue method for furry puppets

- Mark the middle of both the top and lower jaws on both the puppet and the mouthpiece. Align the puppet mouth fabric with the center marks of the mouthpiece.
- Hot glue the center of the puppet's bottom jaw/lip fabric to the mouthpiece in the center bottom jaw (it's that spot between the two front teeth again).
- Moving quickly, and in small segments, run a thin bead of hot glue on the rim of the felted side of the mouthpiece and roll the puppet's mouth fabric up, over, and onto the glue. Hold until cool and firm. Do not move to the next segment until the glue is cool and the hold is solid. Move from the center out to the corners of the mouth, testing the fit and adjusting as needed as you go. Repeat on top jaw/lip.

A BIT CONGESTED IN THERE?

If you are using a Stuffet instead of a custom creation, consider de-stuffing the head for ample hand movement.

11 Add exterior felt mouth details if desired (e.g., uvula or tongue). For a toothier option, see "Adding Teeth" on page 81.

mouth detail examples:

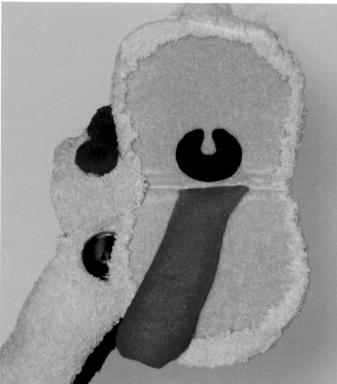

12 If needed, fill the head with batting (that's the non-edible variety of stuffing).

We don't recommend the Thanksgiving Day variety for puppet making. To keep stuffing in place—once you have figured out the placement and quantity—you can bag it up in a nylon stocking and tack it in with a few discreet stitches.

FLOPPY FINGERS

Is your hand constantly slipping around inside the puppet? Sandwich your fingers inside by adding stuffing, foam, or a finger-encasing loop. More examples can be found in the Advanced Puppet-Making Workshop.

option 3: shaped sheet foam puppet mouthpiece

This option is a foam-encased, easily gripped mouthpiece, best used (surprise, surprise) with the Shaped Sheet Foam Puppet head.

supplies

- Hand Puppet Tool Kit
- Plastic or other flexible-but-firm and easy-to-cut mouthpiece material
- Adhesive (contact cement or spray adhesive)
- Tape (cloth-backed or gaffers tape)
- Poly foam sheet
- Felt
- Scrap felt or fabric

YES, FOR THE THIRD TIME!

Remember: be cautious—various adhesives are not only messy but also toxic in the extreme. I can't say it enough—and really, this is only the third time so far—follow all manufacturers' guidelines.

directions

1 Fold the mouthpiece material of your choice in half and slide the fold into the puppet's mouth opening.

2 Trace the puppet's bite radius onto the mouthpiece material.

3 Cut out the mouthpiece material slightly larger than the tracing. Test the fit. Trim in increments until the fit is just about perfect . . . or as perfect as puppet-making and creative endeavors get.

4 Cut the mouthpiece in half at the fold. Tape the two halves of the mouthpiece together with gaffer's tape or another heat-resistant, flexible, cloth-backed tape; leave a 1/4-inch gap in the hinge for ease of movement.

5 Ball up foam or felt remnants to fit underneath your fingers as a grip. Cut a circle of thin, stretchy fleece or another non-slick (you don't want silk, rayon, or any other slippery material here) fabric remnant to cover the rolled up fabric ball. Mark a good finger-gripping location on the mouthpiece material. Stretch the fabric over the ball and, using the fabric to hold the ball in place, glue the whole thing onto the mouthpiece material over your mark.

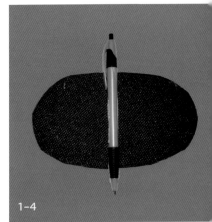

1–4

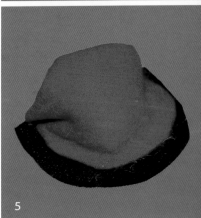

5

6

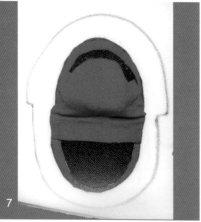

7

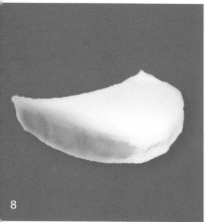

8

9

6 At this point, you can felt the interior of the puppet's mouthpiece. Felting is not necessary if you are reinforcing a fabric mouth.

7 Using the mouthpiece you created in Step 3 as the pattern, cut a slightly larger mouthpiece out of the sheet foam for an encasing cap. The finger-side cap will be slightly larger than the thumb-side cap to accommodate the raised finger grip. Cut the oval in half, as you did for the plastic earlier. Set aside.

8 To make the finger-encasing cap, take half of the foam you cut in Step 7. Spray some adhesive* around the curved edge of the piece. Then spray adhesive around the cut edge of the foam piece. Glue or adhesive should only be placed on the outer 1/2 inch; remove any excess that creeps in further.

   *Contact cement is also an option; it usually takes longer to dry, but there is less overspray.

9 Stick the curved foam edge to the matching curved edges of the top half of the mouthpiece (the side with the finger grip you created in Steps 5 and 6). This creates the foam cap that will keep your fingers from lifting off the mouthpiece as you grip the finger grip. Do not glue the straight-edged or hinged area (the place your fingers slide into). Repeat for bottom foam piece, the side without any finger grip. The thumb portion can be flattened out for a better hold over the thumb. Adjust according to your hand size.

10 Depending on the style of your puppet, you will either:

- Reinforce a sewn mouth by spraying or coating the mouthpiece with adhesive and carefully inserting it up through the puppet head and onto the interior of the mouth. Make sure to adjust the fit before glue dries and

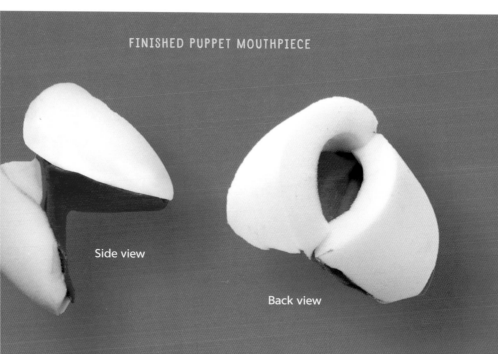

FINISHED PUPPET MOUTHPIECE

Side view

Back view

press firmly around the inside of the mouth to ensure the glued mouthpiece adheres well to either the mouth fabric or foam skull.

- Or, if your puppet has no mouth fabric and the felt of the mouthpiece is what will be visible, roll the puppet's lip fur up and onto the felt and hot glue the mouthpiece into the puppet's mouth opening.

As you gain experience, take it a step further by adjusting the size of the mouthpiece patterns—match and adjust the fabric, foam, and patterns to give your creation a jutting lower lip perfect for nestling a few jagged sharp teeth, or overhang that top lip for the beginnings of a neck-less wonder. Play with frowny faces, or turn it upside down for a greasy grimy gopher gut of a grin.

Congratulations! You now have a fully skinned puppet skull. Take a moment. Pat yourself on the back. The hard part is over. Your naked sheet foam puppet is now ready for upgrades. Proceed to the next section for further puppet embellishments.

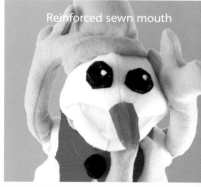

Reinforced sewn mouth

Rolled fabric mouth

MAKING THE TORSO

FOLLOW ALONG IN "FRANKENPUPPET" VIDEO #5

supplies

- Hand Puppet Tool Kit
- Fleece, Vellux®, fur, or other puppet skin* (recycle and use an old fleece coat or blanket)

directions

1 If choosing a low-pile to no-pile skin material for the puppet's torso, fold it in half, right sides together. If you are working with a long-furred material, each side will need to be carefully cut individually. Do not fold the material; instead, trace the pattern (see page 152) on a front and a back piece to cut one by one.

2 Pin the torso pattern along the fold.

3 Cut the fabric pattern out according to the type of skin fabric you've chosen. (See page 35.)

4 If you had to cut long-furred fabric, pin the seams of all fabric pieces back together, keeping the right sides together.

5 Sew the torso fabric into a tube. Check for any missed or popped seams that need to be re-sewn.

6 For the next step, make sure the torso tube is inside out and that the raw seam edges are showing.

7 Now bring in the puppet head you've created so far in Making the Head and Making the Mouth. Remove any foam skull inserts and make sure the puppet's head is turned right side out. Now push the head skin upside down into the torso. Carefully (and liberally) pin the open upper torso to the open neck portion of the head.

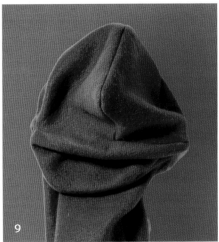

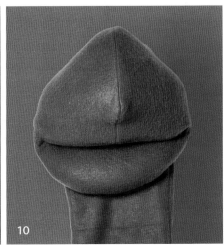

8 Sew the tube to the head, all the way around the pinned neck perimeter.

9 All sewn? Now push the head of the puppet all the way through the bottom of the torso until the entire puppet is right side out. It will look almost finished.

10 Insert the foam skull—if you created one—back into the skin. Adjust, squish, and move the skin around, as needed, until you achieve the desired fit.

The tight fit usually holds the skin on the puppet with no additional glue or sewing.

FOLLOW ALONG IN
"FRANKENPUPPET"
VIDEO #4

MAKING THE HANDS

Elbow, elbow, wrist, wrist. Add two little hands and ta-da! Whether it's a three-fingered hand or a thumb with stitched-for-definition fingers, here are a few ideas to try when making arms and hands.

supplies

- Hand Puppet Tool Kit
- Fleece, Vellux®, fur, or other puppet skin* (recycle and use an old fleece coat or blanket)

directions

1 After choosing your skin material, fold it in half, right sides together.

2 Pin the arm pattern (see pages 150 and 151) along the fold. Pin hand pattern on the still-folded material.

3 Cut out skin and hand patterns using directions in previous sections according to the type of skin fabric you've chosen. Reposition and refold fabric as necessary, and cut the second arm and hand.

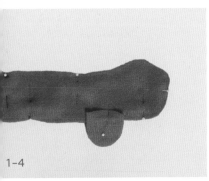

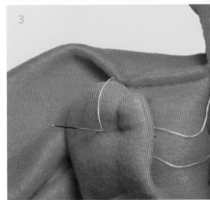

4 Pin seams of all fabric pieces, keeping the right sides together of both arms and hands, including the rod pocket.*

   The rod pocket can be from the same material as the arm and hand, or an alternate material as shown in the video.

5 Sew each arm tube, rod pocket, and hand. Check for any missed or popped seams that need to be re-sewn.

6 Turn each arm/hand right side out.

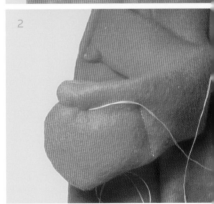

7 Stuff the hands and arms with batting or leftover stuffing—again, the non-edible, non-Thanksgiving variety—leaving gaps for easier wrist and elbow bending. Not enough definition for you? Add a few hand stitches to the elbows and/or wrists, or run them through the sewing machine to emphasize those joints.

mitten-style hand

1 Using heavy-duty or quilting thread, start at the base of the thumb joint. Pull thread through and knot by taking a few stitches in place.

2 Loop thread up over the top of the thumb tip and down the opposite side. Insert the needle into the base of the thumb joint, coming up through the knot. Pull tight enough to create the suggestion of a thumb, but not so tight that you snap your thread. Repeat for two to three more loops. Take a few more stitches in place to secure.

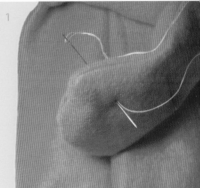

3 Insert the needle between the fabric layers, running it through the batting inside the hand, near the base of the next finger. Bring the needle back up at the base of the finger. Repeat the looping you did for the thumb, and knot it off by stitching several stitches on top of each other.

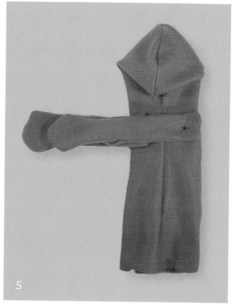

Finished torso with head and arms

TIP:

Use optional doll joints for a full range of motion when attaching shoulder and hip joints.

4 Repeat for the next two fingers. Yes, three fingers and one thumb: the unofficial official thumb-to-finger ratio given to the puppet and cartoon variety of characters. Feel free to deviate, as we creative folk are prone to do.

5 With the tube seam in the back and the fabric right side out, fold the tube flat to mark the arm placement. Cut arm opening slits down from the top of the tube. Insert each arm and hand- or machine-sew the slit back up. Remember: thumbs point up.

knees and toes

Adding feet to your puppet? Put your best foot forward with the pattern found on page 151. Follow the same instructions as used for the arms and hands, using the leg and foot patterns instead.

Congratulations! You now have a naked puppet. Feel free to embellish and personalize your puppet as desired. This is your blank canvas, your pre–magnum opus that awaits only the unleashing of your creative genius.

But wait; does the plethora of possibilities leave you overwhelmed and creatively blocked? Never fear, my fellow ADHD-challenged puppet makers (that is, if you are anything like some of us here on the *Naked Hand* crew). Now that you have addressed the naked hand, let's dress the naked puppet.

MAGNA . . . MAJAS . . . MAGNES-WHAT?

YOUR MAJESTERIAL HIGHNESS WILL DO JUST FINE, YOUNG MAN.

EARS AND EYES

creating a face

While it is true that anything goes in the creation of puppet faces, it's good to know where to begin.

GENERAL RULES OF FACE

1 Center eyes between the crown of the head and the chin, level with the tops of the ears.

2 The ears extend about halfway between eye level and the chin.

3 The bottom of the nose is level with the bottom of the ears.

4 The face overall is about five eyes wide.

5 The outer edges of the nose base should be in line with the centers of the eyes.

6 The hairline comes down about a third of the way between the crown of the head and the eyebrows.

7 Mouth placement is one eye width down from the nose.

BUT . . .

That said, rules are no substitute for a brain, nor are they a substitute for your highly developed sense of artistic style. It's rules, schmules—particularly in puppet building—so get cracking, maestro! Time's a-wasting, and the true fun is just beginning.

FOLLOW ALONG IN
"FRANKENPUPPET"
VIDEO #6

MAKING THE EYES

CAUTION:

Most of these eye options can pose a safety threat to children too young to know that puppets are not chew toys, so be sure to keep these out of reach.

EYE-DEAS

Craft foam fastened with a black two-part safety eye makes a simple eye. So do buttons and wooden beads!

possible supplies

- Plastic spoons
- Felt adhesive furniture protection dots
- Ping-Pong® balls
- Bouncy balls
- Pull-apart plastic Christmas ornaments
- Wooden beads
- Foam practice golf balls
- Plastic Easter eggs
- Acrylic paints
- Two-part safety eyes
- Permanent markers
- Acrylic paints (and brushes)
- Fabric
- Craft foam
- False eyelashes

In short: what isn't an eye? If it resembles an eye in any way, or you think you can turn it into an eye-ish shape, try it. Depending on your eye material, you will want to paint, glue, cut, craft, and create your eye of choice.

- Plastic spoons are a great go-to. Just cut off the handle end and attach a foam dot pupil and a felt eyelid.
- Foam practice golf balls or bouncy balls that have been cut in half (and painted, if desired) are an easy, bulgy-eyed alternative.
- Plastic Christmas ornament balls are a good post-holiday option. Just sand the finish off and spray with a flat-finish, plastic-adhering paint.
- Cut a circle of felt and run a basting stitch around the entire perimeter. Pull the string enough to gather the felt into a round ball and add stuffing to give it shape. Finish it off by pulling the thread tight and stitching directly onto the puppet before tying the thread off in a knot.
- Safety eyes are found in most craft and hobby stores, both brick-and-mortar and virtual online stores. Pierce a hole; push the post of the eye through the fabric of the puppet face and then push on the safety back from inside the puppet head.
- Cut a Ping-Pong® ball in half by piercing a hole in the ball with the sharp end of a pair of scissors and then cutting around the seam once you can insert the scissors into the Ping-Pong® ball. Or leave it whole, pierce a small hole, and attach a safety eye before hot gluing to the puppet. Or paint a pupil with a variety of permanent marker colors. Or even just hot glue a felt dot to it.
- Plastic Easter egg halves can be used just like the Ping-Pong® ball halves, although a hot glue gun (without using any glue) might be needed to burn a hole, as this plastic is a little more brittle.

Embellish the eyes with furry, fuzzy, or even just plain funky eyebrows and eyelids to your heart's delight.

PING PONG
BALLS

PLASTIC
SPOONS

PLASTIC CHRISTMAS
ORNAMENT BALLS

FOAM PRACTICE
GOLF BALLS PLUS
SAFETY EYES

SAFETY EYES

1–5

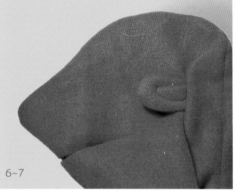

6–7

A CHEEKY TIP:

To get that perfect bashful flush, consider an artful application of chalk or powder blush on those puppet cheeks.

MAKING THE EARS

FOLLOW ALONG IN "FRANKENPUPPET" VIDEO #7

If all your puppet does is talk, talk, talk, maybe it's time to give him or her a hint and put on some ears. What's the old Epictetus quote? "We have two ears and one mouth so that we can listen twice as much as we speak." Wise words, my puppet friend. Wise, indeed.

supplies

- Hand Puppet Tool Kit
- Fleece, Vellux®, fur, or other puppet skin* (recycle and use an old fleece coat or blanket)

directions

1 Using the basic puppet ear pattern on page 151, pin the pattern to the folded piece of right-side-in fabric.

2 With the fabric right side in, cut fabric.

3 Pin the fabric, keeping right sides together.

4 Sew around the ear, leaving the base (the part that attaches to the head) open.

5 Turn the ear right side out.

6 Sew any desired detail into the ear. Stuff before sewing if you wish for a puffier ear.

7 Locate and mark the ear area on your puppet's head. Are your ears even? Do they hang low? Do they wobble to and fro? Can you throw them over your shoulder like a Continental soldier? In other words, check your ear placement. Pinch a fold of fabric from the head and sew the ear onto the fold by hand.

8 Repeat for the other ear.

take the face further:

Our faces are not flat, and your puppet's face doesn't have to be either. Using leftover fleece, fur, or fabric scraps, start building character by sewing wrinkles and other facial features. Sew a ridge above the eyes for a brow. Plump up those cheeks with more than just a beauty mark. Add a bit of stuffing and work wonders. Make your stitches visible in the extreme, à la Frankenstein's monster, or go invisible with minuscule nips and tucks worthy of the finest plastic surgeon. It's all good—and terribly addicting.

WIGS, HAIR PIECES, MUSTACHES, AND MORE

GET IDEAS IN "FRANKENPUPPET" VIDEO #8

While it is fun and easy to simply buy a good wig, it can get a bit pricey. Before you go to the expense, try your hand at these budget-wise alternatives.

simple sewn yarn hair

1 Measure desired length of yarn from the crown to the ends, be it chin length, shoulder length, or '60s hippie.

2 Loop yarn back and forth, twice the length you measured. Find and mark the middle.

3 Lay a strip of matching felt on the center line.

4 Carefully, flip the yarn and felt so that the felt is now on the bottom (so that it runs through a sewing machine without snagging). Sew the yarn to the felt. This has now become the crown, or the part, in the hairpiece.

5 Hand stitch the crown piece to the puppet head.

6 Cut the looped ends of the wig, or give 'em a salon-worthy haircut.

7 Embellish at will with beads, braids, leather, feathers, bands, and bows—just maybe not all at once.

ADD CHARACTER TO YOUR CHARACTER

You can use yarn scraps to make a smaller version of the sewn yarn wig above for a mustache, sideburns, eyebrows, or even that hairy old mole. Still got some bits to use up? Don't toss it. Give your puppet instant age by tucking the remainders into ears and nostrils. It's all character—right?

1–3

4

5

THIS LOOKS KIND OF FAMILIAR.

easy fuzzy fabric hair

1 Measure the scalp area of your puppet.

2 Choose a likely fuzzy fabric and cut a large circle to fit your measurements.

3 Cut strips from the outer edges to the center circle—leaving un-cut the crown area that holds it all together. It should look like a big sun with rays of light emanating out from the center when you are done.

4 Cut out a few darts to make the piece fit nicely over the rounded puppet head. Test the fit, then hand stitch the darts closed.

5 Hot glue or hand stitch the hairpiece to the puppet.

FUR WORKS TOO!

Instead of a fuzzy fabric, use fur. Just remember, when cutting your sun-with-rays shape, cut along the base of the fur strands so that the fur flows freely instead of being scalped short. Refer to medium- to long-pile fur-cutting tips on page 35.

STAND DOWN, MATEY. YE'LL NEED A SHIPLOAD OF HAIR BEFORE GETTIN' DREADS LIKE ME OWN.

BLUE SCRUBBY

FUZZY FABRIC

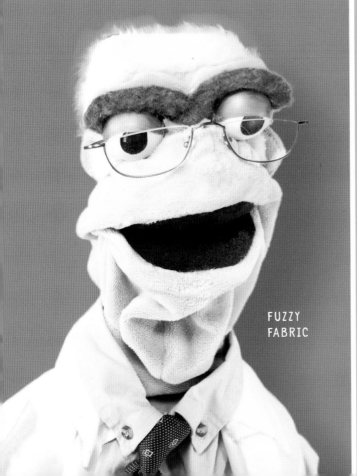

FUZZY FABRIC

even easier hair ideas

- Grab a dollar-store scrubby or duster. Trim as needed, and sew or glue it onto your puppet.
- Glue in a few feathers or part of a feather boa.

FEATHER BOA

COSTUMING

It's time to get some clothing on this poor puppet. Let's do it with some style! What to wear . . . and what not to wear? Okay, okay, there really isn't much a puppet can't pull off. Maybe. Let your creativity out of the box when dressing your puppet. Literally. Although you can use a box if you want to.

where to shop

- Secondhand stores
- Garage sales
- Raiding mom's saved and treasured baby clothes . . . or maybe not

what to get

- Old baby clothing
- Children's clothing, typically sizes 2–4
- Socks
- Shoes
- Eyeglasses, sunglasses, or goggles
- Hats
- Belts, feathers, beads, and more

These puppets can be a slippery bunch. It's the happy puppeteer (and happier audience) who attaches the clothing to the puppet with a few firm yet discreet stitches. No naked shows allowed. We are a family-oriented bunch, after all.

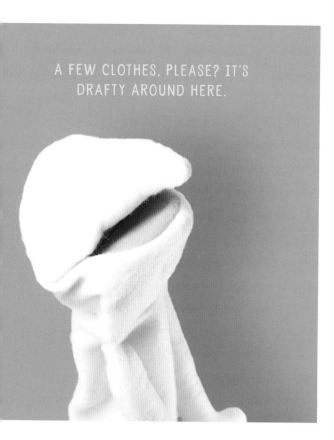

A FEW CLOTHES, PLEASE? IT'S DRAFTY AROUND HERE.

THE FIX FOR BAGGY CLOTHES

If your puppet is on the small side, or your preferred article of clothing is a bit big, just turn the piece inside out, tuck in those shoulder and side seams—pinning and test fitting as you go—and sew new shoulder and/or side seams to fit.

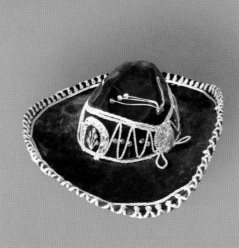

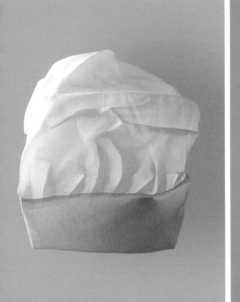

STRIKE IT BIG

Halloween is your time, my friend. It's a great opportunity to pick up wigs, accessories, and more. If you wait until the post-holiday sales, well, you just scored big time. The hardest part will be holding yourself in check and sticking to your budgeted allowance.

BUT, BUT, WHAT ABOUT *CHRISTMAS?*

chapter 3

ADVANCED PUPPET WORKSHOP

GETTING STARTED

Finding that your puppet is a bit of a stuffed shirt? A little lacking in character? Do you feel a desperate need to get up and get moving? If so, it's time you learned how to give your puppet creations a bit more individuality.

advanced tool kit

A   Scissors—the good pair for the fabrics

B   Scissors—the craft pair that still cut fairly well

C   Wooden spoon or dowel

D   Permanent markers in a variety of colors

E   Utility knife (breakaway blade, carpet blade, and/or razor blade)

F   Self-healing cutting mat

G   Foam brushes, if using contact cement (or a scrap of foam as a make-do brush)

H   Pencil

I   Hot glue gun and glue sticks (optional)*

J   Sewing pins

K   Paintbrushes (a variety)

L   Sewing machine and thread

M   Needle and quilting or heavy-duty thread

N   Protective eyewear

O   Rubber gloves

P   Electric (turkey) knife

Q   Rasp

R   Razor

S   Rotary sanding tool (like a Dremel®)

Ventilation mask, one for toxic fumes (not just particulates or organic odors)

The best glues and adhesives have a strong, flexible bond.

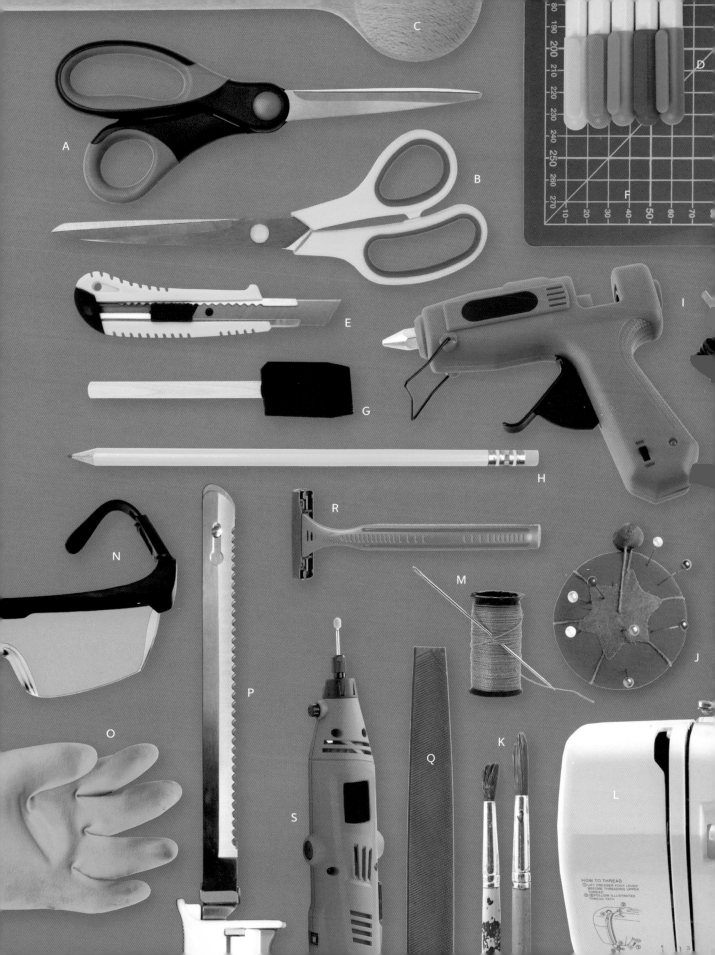

PERSONALIZED SHEET FOAM PUPPET

Got a great puppet shape idea in your head? Don't know where to get that customized pattern? Make your own patterns from objects readily at hand.

YOU CAN ALSO MAKE A PATTERN FROM CLAY

Maybe you have a hankering for some clay play. Pulling a puppet pattern from your own personal clay sculpture is not only fun but also a sure-fire way to create your own custom puppet designs.

FOAM CHOICES

The three types of foam generally used in puppet making are:

- Reticulated foam, or dry lux open-cell foam. It comes in different PPIs (pores per square inch); 35 PPI seems to be the magic number, but sample different types to find your preference. This kind of foam is commonly used in filters (fish and vacuum).
- Closed-cell foam, specifically L200. This foam holds its shape well and is lightweight.
- Poly foam. This is the foam you most commonly see in your local craft and fabric stores.

Caveat: choose objects that are already well used and even unloved—something like an old basketball or, better yet, an object that no one will cry tears over if it is damaged. Now scour your local regions—home, office, or garage. Find your perfect shape.

supplies

- Advanced Tool Kit
- Packaging tape (duct or masking tape work well, too)
- Item with shape of choice
- Sheet foam, 1/2–1 inch thick for L200 or reticulated open cell foam or 1–2 inches thick for poly foam
- Fabric skin of choice
- Foam of choice: closed cell L200, reticulated open cell, or poly foam (see sidebar)
- Adhesive glue of choice (contact cement or spray)
- Large piece of paper or poster board
- Mouthpiece of choice

directions

1 Cover the object with one or two layers of tape—sticky side OUT.

2 Go over it again, this time with the sticky side IN, until the entire shape has been covered. No sticky-side-out tape should be left uncovered. You might need a few extra layers.

3 Look over your object, noticing the ridges, the valleys, and the curves. Also decide on the mouth placement. You will want to make your cuts in the next step with mouth placement and best seam placements in mind.

4 Locate likely seams and carefully cut the tape shape off the item along those seams. Lay tape pattern flat. If there are any bumps, flatten them by cutting in a dart. Trace the newly flattened tape shapes onto the large piece of paper or poster board. Your tape pattern is now ready to be traced onto your foam sheet.

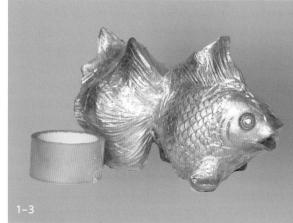
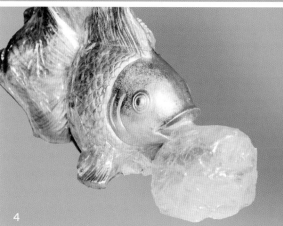

1–3

4

TAKE YOUR TIME

Take copious notes as you trace the taped shapes onto the paper. Color code—using permanent markers—the edges/seams that should join to each other (e.g., blue to blue). Or label the pattern with letters instead of a color (e.g., side A on the body matches up to side A on the head piece). It's also a good idea to measure the matching seams to make sure they truly do match up. Adjust your tracings accordingly.

BE PATIENT WITH YOURSELF

As with most art forms, this technique takes some practice. Trial and error are a part of the process. Just remember: there are no mistakes, only challenges in disguise.

5 Lay the paper pattern on the sheet foam. Trace around it with a permanent marker.

6 Label each foam piece with an identifying name and directional arrows (e.g., up vs. down) so that you can reassemble the foam after it is cut.

7 Cut out the foam pattern with either the breakaway blade on a self-healing cutting mat or the not-so-good scissors.

8 Glue foam shape together with either spray adhesive or contact cement. If all goes well, it should resemble the object you used to make your pattern. If not, you can start over or just go with the flow.

9 Using your paper pattern from Step 4, add 1/4-inch to 1/2-inch seam allowances. Consider altering some seam locations for an optimally fitting skin. Hide your seams whenever possible.

10 Choose a skin fabric.

11 Pin your paper pattern to the skin fabric you've chosen. Don't forget your seam allowances.

12 Cut the fabric, following the shape of the pattern. If you are using fur, follow the fur-cutting instructions on page 140 in the Resources section.

13 Remove the paper pattern from the skin material. Keeping the fabric inside out, pin and sew the darts.

14 Starting with the head, sew the puppet shape together in an orderly and planned fashion.

15 Move from the head to the body portion and sew the remainder of the skin. Sew the center seams, remembering to leave an adequate puppeteer hand opening. If you have a uniquely shaped puppet, you might have to play it by ear while sewing. Remember: a rule is not substitute for a brain.

16 Decide what kind of mouthpiece you wish to create for the puppet: sewn in, sewn reinforced, or hot glued. Refer back to the Hand Puppet Workshop on page 45 for a refresher course, if needed. Or, hold off until you reach the Advanced Mouthpalate section coming up soon on page 77 for additional options.

17 Insert the foam skull (and body, if a body was part of your design) into the skin. The tight fit usually holds the skin on the puppet with no additional glue or sewing. Hand sew any additional seams where necessary. Spray adhesive or contact cement is a good go-to if your puppet's skin is fitting a bit too loosely. Spray or spread the adhesive on the foam, then pull on the skin. Press firmly to get adhesion.

18 After inserting and sewing or gluing in the finished mouthpiece, embellish your puppet with facial features, hair, and costuming as desired.

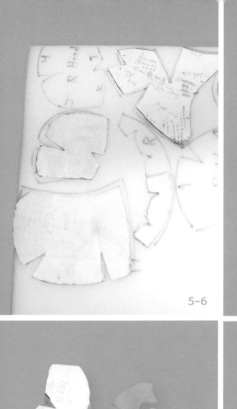

5-6

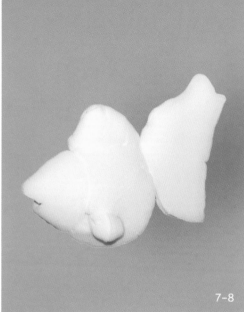

7-8

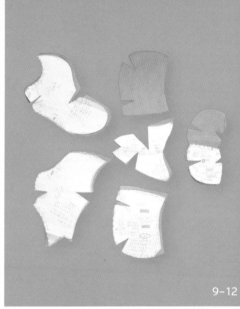

9-12

13

14

15

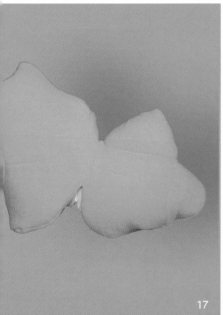

17

18

LEARN ALL ABOUT FOAM
IN "ADVANCED PUPPET
WORKSHOP" VIDEO #1

CARVED FOAM BLOCK PUPPET

Carry on, my fine, furry, hairy friends! Break into the big leagues with these super skills. And soon, you shall be the envy of all who surround you.

A NOTE ABOUT MATERIALS:

*The main type of foam used here is polyurethane, what we refer to as poly foam—it is a couch cushion foam. It comes in many varieties and densities. Foam can usually be purchased in sheets or blocks.

**Watered down Mod Podge® or most any water-soluble glue can be used as a fabric stiffener.

supplies

- Advanced Tool Kit
- Adhesive glue (contact cement or spray adhesive)
- Block foam*
- Long sewing pins
- Mouthpiece of choice
- Muslin or other lightweight cotton (non-stretchy) fabric
- White glue** (mixed half and half with water)
- Permanent markers
- Puppet skin fabric of choice (optional)

directions

1 Plan a puppet image or shape. Sketch the idea out. Include a profile, or side view, and a front view with the puppet's face straight on.

2 Using a permanent marker, sketch the character's profile (the side-view) onto the side of the block of foam.

SKETCHING TIP:

If you have access to a gooseneck projector, draw your design onto a piece of transparent plastic or a store-bought transparency sheet. Project the drawn image, using the gooseneck projector, onto a wall. Hold the block of foam against the wall. Eyeball the dimensions, and move the projector forward or back to adjust for size. Trace the patterns onto the foam. Face forward first, trimming the foam down to size as needed, then repeat for the profile.

profile view

front view

3 Sketch the front view on the front of the block of foam. Make sure it fits in place with the previously drawn profile.

4 Using an electric knife—or a serrated knife, if electric is not an option—cut a smaller block (the size of your puppet head) from your big foam block around the edges of your sketched outlines.

5 Now that you have a profile and a front view traced onto the foam, and a manageable cut-down foam block, start paring down the shape to more closely match your sketch with the serrated or electric knife. You may find it necessary, depending on your eyeballing abilities, to also sketch and trace a from-the-top-of-the-head view onto the foam block.

CAUTION:

When cutting, BE CAREFUL! Not only are the blades sharp, but you also want to be sure not to undercut any of the sides (e.g., you accidentally cut a 120-degree angle when what you needed was a 90-degree angle). Go slowly, and be deliberate with every cut.

6 When you can no longer safely cut with the large knife, start snipping at the rough corners and edges with a pair of craft scissors. Cut off any ridges and edges that you want smoothed out. Snip away with the scissors until nothing but some fine-tuning is needed.

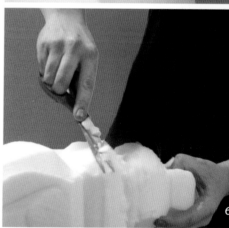

CAN I TRY
IT NOW?

BEWARE THE PERILS OF ELECTRIC SANDING

Spinning disc sanders and foam are uncomfortable when in close proximity. The foam will grab onto the sander at the most inopportune of times and suck the spinning blade deep into its recesses. It's a surefire way to sabotage a puppet sculpture, file off an uncomfortable layer of skin, and even fling said sanders across the work room.

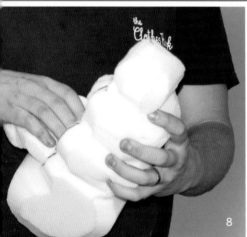

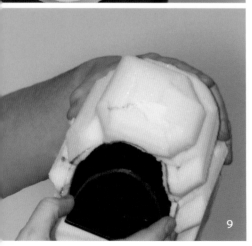

7 Sand off any remaining rough spots with the rasp, or, if you dare, using EXTREME CAUTION, you can try using the electric sander.

8 If you have not already made a bottom jaw, either (a) cut a foam jaw from the almost-finished sculpture with a long serrated knife or (b) sketch and cut a jaw from the original block of foam using Steps 1–8.

9 Create a pre-skin mouthpiece using your choice of mouthpiece instructions in the book. Or, depending on your creative muse, you can wait to add the mouthpiece until the foam is tightly encased in a skin of your own making.

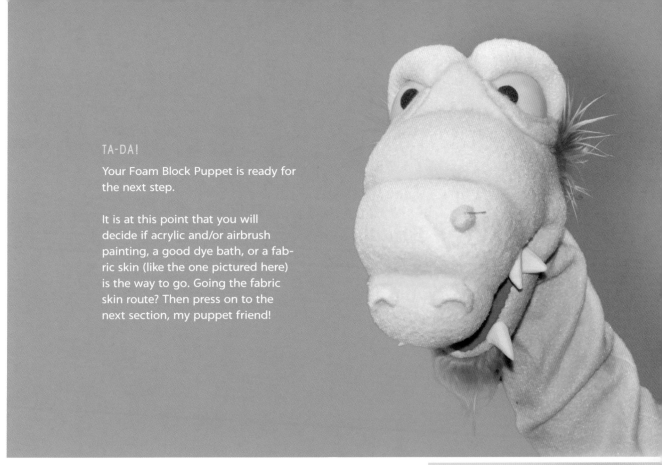

TA-DA!

Your Foam Block Puppet is ready for the next step.

It is at this point that you will decide if acrylic and/or airbrush painting, a good dye bath, or a fabric skin (like the one pictured here) is the way to go. Going the fabric skin route? Then press on to the next section, my puppet friend!

CREATING THE FABRIC SKIN PATTERN

1 Cover the foam head with a wet piece of muslin or other lightweight cotton fabric. Make the top and bottom jaws separately.

2 Pinch excess fabric up into wedges. Stick pins through the fabric and into the foam to hold fabric in place wherever it is needed.

3 Brush the mixture of half white glue and half water over the fabric. Let dry.

4 Look over your object: notice the ridges, the valleys, and the curves while it dries. You already have a mouth location and lower jaw; you just need to decide on the rest of the needed seams.

5 Remove the dry and stiffened fabric from the foam shape, cutting seams as you go, if needed.

6 Lay out the fabric, and flatten any bumps by cutting in darts.

7 Mark the edges/seams that will join together (e.g., side A with side A).

Starting piece

1–3

4

8 Choose a skin fabric.

9 Pin the fabric pattern to your chosen skin material. Leaving those seam allowances—1/4 inch to 1/2 inch—reconsider any seam locations and move them now for an ideal-fitting skin. It's a brilliant puppeteer who can hide the seams.

10 Cut the fabric, using the pattern as a guide. If using fur, follow the fur-cutting instructions on page 140 in the Resources section.

11 Remove the paper pattern from the skin material before sewing. Keep labeling those pieces to eliminate confusion in the assembly. You might also consider keeping the pieces laid out in the order of assembly, abutting seams to seams as a visual reminder of what needs sewing when and to where.

12 With the right sides of the fabric together, pin the darts and sew the darts together.

13 Pin the larger sides of the fabric pieces together and sew the remaining seams of the skin. You might have a few more than the simple up-over-the-head and down-under-the-chin seams, but if you've made it this far in the book, you can do it.

14 If your puppet is still lacking a mouth, measure, cut, and sew in the mouth fabric.

LABELING IS YOUR FRIEND

Color code or alpha code as mentioned in the Personalized Sheet Foam Puppet segment. Consider labeling all the pattern pieces with the name of the puppet. It never hurts to save each of your patterns in large envelopes. Clear labeling and lots of instructions go a long way toward making a duplicate puppet re-creation work.

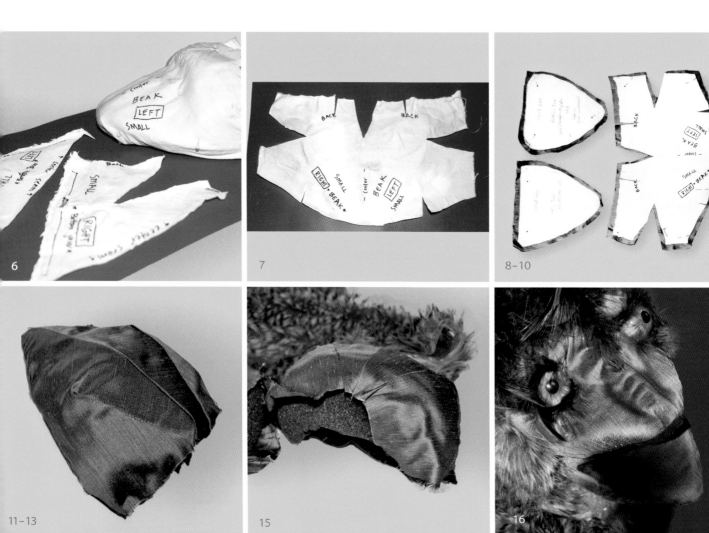

6

7

8–10

11–13

15

16

This step might take a few trials, as every shape and resulting mouth has really and truly been hand-designed by you. Refer back to the Stuffet Hinged Mouthpiece section or the Shaped Sheet Foam instructions in the Hand Puppet Workshop for a refresher course if you need it, 'cause, you know, sometimes we all do. Or move forward into the Advanced Mouthpalate Tutorial that follows.

15 Insert foam block head (and body, if a body was part of your design) into the skin.

16 After inserting and sewing in (gluing is also an option) the finished mouthpiece, embellish your puppet with facial features, hair, and costuming as desired.

alternate skin ideas

- Painting foam is always an option. Paint doesn't last as long as the fabric alternatives, but it does give you an additional creative outlet. Mixing rubber latex into your typical inexpensive acrylic paints will add flexibility to your painting. It will still crack and peel, eventually. If painting becomes your preferred method of covering a foam construction, consider experimenting with silicon pigment paints available at specialty shops, such as those found at Smooth-on.com.
- Not into painting? Grab some fabric dye, mix up a nice batch (following the manufacturer's directions), and dunk that foam carving. This is best done after all the carving is complete, as foam does not dye uniformly. The insides will invariably be different shades of dark or light. Once you have reached your desired color, squeeze and squeeze to get as much water out of the foam as possible. Now set it aside. It's going to take a while to dry out.
- Or blend a bit of all of the above: fabric, paint, and dye.

YOU WOULD TELL ME IF MY ROOTS WERE SHOWING . . . RIGHT?

MAKE IT A MONSTER . . . OR ANOTHER CREATURISTIC CREATION OF THE ROAAARING TYPE

Using most any pattern, replace that fleece with some fuzzy, fun faux fur. Mix and match the eyes. Add true-to-life animal snouts, or go for a funky beaked nose complete with a warty old chin. Even better, experiment with fabrics and materials. Next, try your hand at sewing on character-building facial features. There really is no wrong way, and besides, a monstrous creation is a perfect project for masking a beginner's trials and errors.

EXPANDABLE FOAM PUPPET

Really want to go out on a limb with a unique foam puppet? Try your hand at making lightweight, expandable foam creations.

*Extreme caution must be employed when using spray foams. Amateurs have been known to overfill and burst walls with this stuff—not to mention the extreme stickiness that can result from overuse of an almost never-ending, ever-expanding product.

HAVE A FOUNDATION

**Foam core won't warp, but plan on having a permanent piece of foam core embedded in your creature. Poster board will warp, but it can also be ripped off the dried creation. Both work well.

supplies

- Advanced Tool Kit
- Spray insulating foam sealant*
- Foam core or poster board**
- Packing tape (for reinforcing or making custom boxes; optional)
- Cardboard boxes (optional)

Despite the cautions, you might consider this form of puppet making very rewarding. If so, go with the flow and try your hand at this lightweight and extremely satisfying method of growing your puppet menagerie (pun intended). Go free flowing and easy with the foam-core method, or go downright structured by filling a box or other custom-built foam container shapes. In either case, it's time to let your inner artist loose.

directions

1 If you are just starting out, try spraying a splot of foam onto a large foam core or poster board base. It is highly suggested that you test the expansion rate of your foam first. Try it somewhere safe and, well, somewhere large and sans any household pests—er, I mean pets—with lots of space, just in case.

SPRAY IT SMART

It's highly recommended that you use the entire can of expandable foam all at once, not on just one puppet, but on multiple puppet starts. Lay out multiple poster or foam core boards and spray it all out. Don't plan on completing one large creation in one fell swoop; if you start going too big, you will soon find that wet spray foam does not stick to wet spray foam. It is a slippery and deceptively slimy substance. To build on a creation, you will need to hold a second spray session with a second can of spray foam, wherein you build up newly sprayed foam onto an already dry puppet start.

2 Let the foam dry according to the manufacturer's recommendation. Take the intervening time to imagine a face, a shape, an image. Not unlike the inkblot test in the psych ward, it's a great time to get in touch with that inner Rorschach self of yours.

3 At this point, you should decide whether your creation's skin texture is fabulous as is or whether you want to carve and sand it down.

4 If all it needs is a great coat of paint, paint away using either acrylic paints with a brush, spray paint, or airbrushing—or even a combination of them all—then skip to Step 8.

5 If you are carving, start carving with breakaway blades and/or a serrated knife. Careful, there! Do I need to remind you exactly how sharp knives are? Maybe I should mention that this kind of foam slices like the creamy butter its color resembles.

Keep carving.

Carve a little more. I know. Takes a while, doesn't it? Messy, too.

6 Sand a little with the rasp; maybe get the rotary sander into it a bit. A ventilation mask and goggles are highly recommended at this point.

7 If you have been custom carving, make sure you have carved the top of the head (upper lip to the crown). Also consider the addition of a few more splots of foam to either the carved or the natural un-carved face. Or consider adding some additional expanding foam to the back of the foam core for roundness. Carve the back of the head if desired, after it's dry, of course.

8 Prep the puppet for a mouthpiece by cutting off the bottom jaw.

9 Make your mouthpiece of choice and glue it in. Your stickiest of sticky glue is highly useful in this step, as the foam tends to crumble a bit if overly stressed.

10 Add a body sleeve, or at least a neck. Glue the sleeve to the back of the head—using the uber-sticky stuff down around the side of the head—and attach to the bottom jaw. Sometimes an additional coating of hot glue is advised to make sure your head and neck, or body, stay together.

11 Add poly foam, L200, or covered reticulated open cell foam constructions and shapes for added facial features as desired.

2

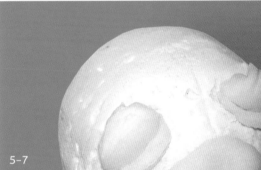

5–7

8

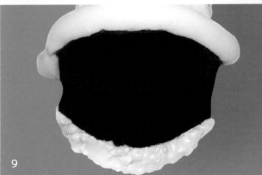

9

10–11

finish options

- Paint with a latex-and-acrylic paint mixture.
- Add facial features like teeth, eyes, warts and more. If your spray can sputtered a bit at the tail end of the spray session, save those little dollops and drips; they make great warts and cankerous growths that are considered one of the most desirable of beauty marks in the troll and monster fashion world.
- Spray paint. Add brushed-on acrylic paints to gain depth and color variations.

- Already a pro painter? Experiment with highly rewarding airbrush painting.
- Use a carved spray foam form as a shape from which to pull a fabric pattern in the same way demonstrated in the Personalized Sheet Foam Puppet or the Carved Foam Block Puppet sections. It almost goes without saying, but you will omit the sheet foam cutting steps and only use the tape or cotton/muslin pattern for the fabric skin.

WASN'T THAT FUN?
There really isn't anything greater than a creative high. Take a moment and bask in your creative glory.

Done basking? Good.

Now, let's move along . . .

ADVANCED MOUTHPALATES

OPTION 1: THE ADVANCED SOFT MOUTHPALATE

The following mouthpalates are open* when at rest. Many puppeteers prefer a puppet mouth to remain open when at rest, as this helps prevent hand fatigue; it is easier to close your fingers than to open them. The decision on which mouth to use is up to you and your puppet. And honestly, if you are going to be doing a lot of puppeteering, nothing less than a good amount of muscle building will help you in the end.

*See the mouthpiece instructions found in the Stuffet and Hand Puppet Workshops for mouths that are closed when at rest.

supplies

- Advanced Tool Kit
- Heavy-duty plastic that can be cut with scissors or a utility blade
- Sheet polyfoam or reticulated open-cell foam
- Strong adhesive tape such as gaffer's or book binder's tape (tape with heat-resistant adhesive)
- Foam-adhering adhesive (contact cement or spray glue—again, follow all manufacturer cautions)
- Hot glue gun and glue sticks (optional)
- Fleece
- Felt: flesh, red, pink, black, etc.

directions

1 Measure the bite of your prospective puppet by inserting the folded mouthpalate material into the puppet mouth.

2 Trace the puppet's bite with a permanent marker onto the mouthpalate material. Trace both the bottom and top jaws.

3 Cut out the mouthpalate.

4 Cut the mouthpalate in half at the fold—the hinge. If your puppet has equal-sized top and bottom jaws, the cut will be in the middle. If your puppet has a large bottom jaw with a smaller top jaw, or vice versa, cut accordingly.

5 Tape the two pieces together with heat-resistant tape, leaving about a 1/4-inch width of space between for ease of movement. Push the tape deep into the opening so that it adheres to itself when you flip the mouthpalate over and tape the back. Additionally, if you tape while hanging half of the mouthpalate over the

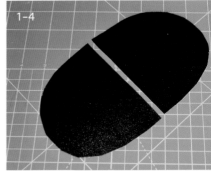

edge of a desk, the resulting taped gap will create a hinge that stays open at a 90-degree angle when at rest.

6 Trace the shape of the mouthpalate onto a piece of sheet foam. Choose your foam wisely; there is a noticeable difference between 1/4-inch foam and 1- to 2-inch foam. If you prefer a very soft, springy mouthpalate, use thicker foam.

7 Cut a foam shape in the exact shape and size of the traced mouthpalate.

8 Glue the foam to one side of the mouthpalate.

9 Trace and cut a 1/2-inch to 1-inch larger mouthpalate shape out of felt. Glue felt or fleece over the foam you have just glued to the mouthpalate; this becomes the visible part of the mouth interior, that is, the part your audience sees when your puppet talks.

10 Again, using your mouthpalate as a pattern, trace out another foam oval, this time adding an extra 1/2 inch. Cut the foam out. Cut foam in half at the hinge. These pieces will be the foam finger caps.

11 Glue foam caps as shown onto the back of the mouthpalate to hold fingers and thumb in place while manipulating the puppet mouth. The finger cap should be rounded up higher than the thumb cap. Flatten the thumb cap down until the foam fits like a nice thumb hug.

OPTION:

Line the interior of the foam caps with fleece to protect the puppeteer's fingers from the deceptively abrasive foam.

OPTION 2: THE ADVANCED HARD MOUTHPALATE

FOLLOW ALONG IN "ADVANCED PUPPET WORKSHOP" VIDEO #2

This custom-made mouthpalate is a delight to work in. Try it out; it's worth the added effort—so much so that we can pretty much guarantee it will be your go-to mouth of choice. Plus, there is a helpful pattern for all its components on page 156.

supplies

- Advanced Tool Kit
- Heavy-duty plastic that can be cut with scissors or a utility blade
- Closed-cell L200 Foam, 1/2 inch thick
- Reticulated open-cell foam, 1/2 inch thick
- Strong adhesive tape such as gaffer's or book binder's tape (tape with heat-resistant adhesive)
- Foam-adhering adhesive (contact cement or spray glue—again, follow all manufacturer cautions)
- Hot glue gun and glue sticks (optional)
- Fleece
- Felt: flesh, red, pink, or black, etc.

directions

1 Follow Steps 1–5 from Option 1, the soft palate: measure, trace, cut out, and tape the hinge of a custom-fitted mouthpalate from the material of your choice. We recommend corrugated plastic for this particular piece. Note that this plastic does not fold well; it's best to trace each jaw individually.

2 Hold the taped mouthpalate in your hand. Find a good holding spot that is comfortable for your hand.

3 With a permanent marker, trace around your fingers and your thumb. Trace out a half circle shape where your fingertips fit. Trace a horseshoe shape around the thumb location.

4 Cut the half circle shape and the horseshoe shape out of 1/2-inch L200 closed-cell foam.

5 Hot glue the foam pieces to the mouthpalate (the circular finger grip on one half of the palate and the thumb horseshoe on the other). The open end of the horseshoe will point toward the wrist; the rounded top will point toward the hinge.

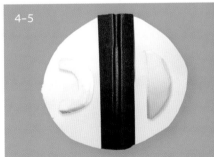

6 Trace the shape of the fully opened mouthpalate onto a scrap piece of fleece. Cut a bit larger than your tracing. Using spray adhesive or contact cement, glue scrap fleece over the grips as shown. Trim excess fleece.

7

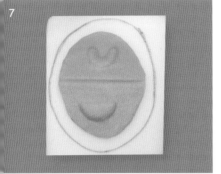

8a

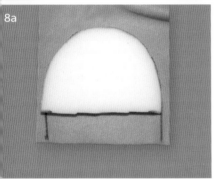

8b

9

10–11

7 Using the opened mouthpalate as a pattern again, trace the palate shape about 1/2 inch larger onto a piece of 1/2-inch reticulated open-cell foam. Cut the foam piece out. Cut it in half at the hinge. Or, if only doing a top cap, you only need the half, not the whole.

8 Cut another piece of soft and stretchy fleece using the foam from Step 7 as a pattern and, using your choice of adhesive, cover all of the foam that will come into contact with the puppeteer's hand with fleece. The fleece will cover all of one side and go up and over the straight edge (hinge cut) of the foam. Repeat for the thumb portion of the foam cap if you are making a thumb cap. Closely trim excess fleece around the curve of the foam.

9 Glue the curved edge of the foam to the companion curved edge of the mouthpalate with contact or spray adhesive.

10 Again, using the fully opened mouthpalate as a pattern, cut a piece of felt—yes, this time it is the less flexible felt we are using, not the stretchy fleece—about 1/2 inch larger than the mouthpalate.

11 Using adhesive, glue the felt to the interior of the mouth (this is the portion of the mouth that is visible to the audience). Be careful to press in the fold first, making sure there are no bumps or unwanted creases. Firmly adhere the remainder of the felt. Wrap the excess 1/2 inch up and onto the foam cap. Cut darts to round the felt up and over the edge of the foam if needed.

ANOTHER EXAMPLE OF A FINISHED MOUTHPALATE

CHOOSE YOUR FELT WELL

This is the interior of the mouth and the part visible to the audience.

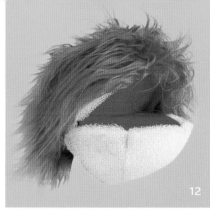

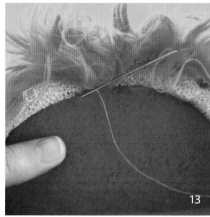

1 2 Glue the mouthpalate into the foam skull of your choice.

1 3 When sewing this mouthpalate to puppet fur, tack the fur in place with small dabs of hot glue. Complete the attachment by hand-sewing the fur to the felt for a more durable and less melt-in-your-hot-vehicle puppet.

Now slip that puppet mouthpalate on your hand. Doesn't it feel good? Comfortable, lightweight, and delightful, isn't it? Worth the work. But then a job well done usually does feel right in the end.

ADDING LIPS

Add some big fat lips by cutting an additional strip of sheet foam, about 1 inch tall by 1 inch wide and long enough to go around the circumference of the mouth perimeter. Begin in a corner of the mouth, and glue the foam strip around the mouthpiece. Cover the foam with felt before gluing, or carve, paint, or dye it to create some truly wonderful and unique puppet lip options.

ADDING TEETH

Using a dense—closed-cell L200—and probably white (yellow teeth are an option, if slightly less savory and a bit more menacing) foam, cut and carve canines, molars, bicuspids, and more until you achieve your puppet-heart's desire.

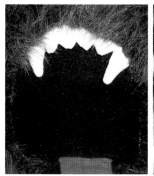

ARM RODS AND ATTACHED HANDS

Attach thin steel round rods (think good, sturdy, hanger-sized wire) or dowels to the puppet's hands for some unparalleled arm control and hand movement.

FOLLOW ALONG IN "ADVANCED PUPPET WORKSHOP" VIDEO #3

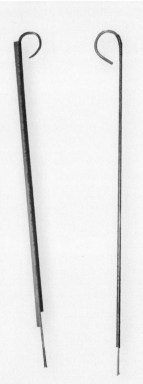

Heat shrink tubing provides a nice protective finish

supplies

- Advanced Tool Kit
- Needle-nose pliers
- Wire-cutting pliers
- Heat gun (your average hair dryer will work in a pinch)
- Permanent marker
- Scissors
- Utility knife
- Hot pad or heat-resistant gloves
- Power drill with 1/8-inch wood drill bit (optional, for wooden handle option)
- Wire, round bar 1/8-inch diameter, approximately 18 inches long per rod
- Heat shrink tubing*, 1/4 inch, black or flat black
- Plastic dip or multipurpose rubber coating spray or dip, black
- Wooden 1-inch round dowel for handle grips, approximately 4–6 inches long per handle (optional, for wooden handle option)
- Wood glue or multipurpose metal/wood adhesive
- Open-cell reticulated foam (optional, for hand shapes)
- Thin, bendable wire, approximately 26 gauge, such as floral wire (optional, for hand shapes)
- Tape (gaffer's, duct, or book binder's—anything with strong adhesive)

directions

1 Using needle-nose pliers, bend the wire just enough to hold the puppet's wrist. If you keep the bend open-ended, you can remove the rods with ease and at will.

2 Slide heat shrink tubing over the rod, then heat shrink with heat gun.

3 Bend the other end of the rod to protect your hand as a handle, or consider straightening and adding a wooden grip.

wooden handgrip option:

1 Follow Steps 1 and 2 in the Arm Rods and Handgrips section. If you are using a hanger, straighten out the human end of the rod (the non-puppet-hand end).

2 Cut the 1-inch wooden dowel into about 5 inch–long segments.

3 Drill a 1 1/2 inch– to 2 inch–deep hole straight down and into one end of the dowel.

4 Insert straightened end of the rod into drilled hole and seal with multipurpose glue. Let dry.

5 Sand dowel as much or as little as desired.

6 Dip wooden handgrip into multipurpose rubber-coating spray or tool coating dip such as Plasti-Dip®. Follow all manufacturer guidelines. Dip far enough to cover the bottom end of the shrink plastic.

A NOTE ON HEAT SHRINK TUBING

*You'll need polyolefin material with a 2:1 shrink ratio, typically used for electrical wires. Match the shrink size to your wire size.

GET CREATIVE

Alternate options include wrapping rods with gripper tape, sanding and painting the rods with a metal coating paint, forming and baking a clay handle, or even leaving as raw wood.

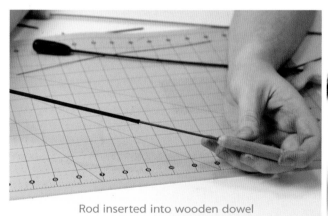

Rod inserted into wooden dowel

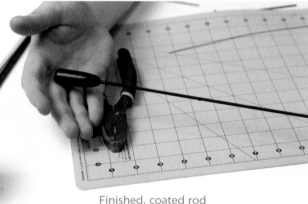

Finished, coated rod

advanced handgrip with attached poseable hand option:

1 Follow the directions in Steps 1–6 in the Wooden Handgrip section.

2 Cut two hand shapes from 1/4- to 1/2-inch reticulated open-cell foam.

3 Twist and wrap thin-gauge wire into the shape of a hand. Match the size to your foam hand cutouts.

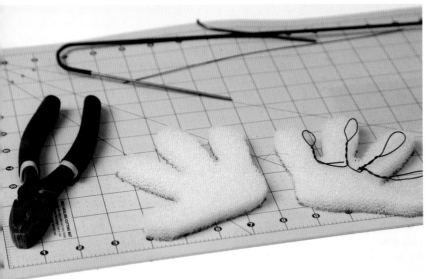

Create multitudes of rods attached to foam hands for a quick grab-and-sew option to finish your puppets with their own personal hands. All it takes is a decision on skin material, the cutting of the hand shape from your chosen fabric, the subsequent stitching of skin onto the foam form, and then the sewing of the finished hand to the puppet wrist.

1–3

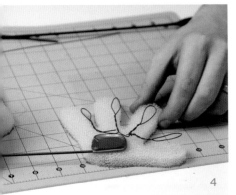

4

4 Bend the top of the rod—the side without the wooden handgrip—in a tight loop. This loop prevents the rod from working its way out of the eventual puppet hand. Tape over this bend. Trim tape around the outside edges.

5 Make a rod/hand sandwich in this order: foam hand, small-gauge wire, rod with taped end, second foam hand. Once you are satisfied with the fit of all the pieces, use contact cement or spray adhesive and glue it all together like a nice BLT on toast. Let dry.

6 To finish the foam hand, spray adhesive along the raw edges of the foam (in between those fingers and around the edge). When glue becomes tacky (as per manufacturer's directions), pinch the edges together, making the seam disappear. This gives the foam fingers a more rounded and natural shape versus the square-finger look you had before.

5

additional options

- Thin wooden dowels wrapped with black electrical tape make for a quick, easy, and low-cost alternative to steel rods. Add hook and loop tape to the puppet end of the rod and pair it up with the rod pocket arm option.
- Cover the bent wrist-wrapping end of a rod with a scrap of puppet skin fabric for a rod that practically disappears on any of your more naked-armed puppets. Use a strong multi-use adhesive, and overlap the fabric on itself to get a good adhesive seal.
- Hot glue the rods into rod pockets or in a less visible wrist spot if you desire a permanent rod solution.

6

GET A HANDLE ON IT WITH THE RIGHT TYPE OF GRIP

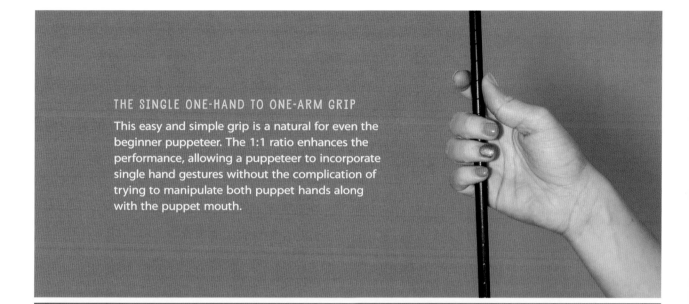

THE SINGLE ONE-HAND TO ONE-ARM GRIP

This easy and simple grip is a natural for even the beginner puppeteer. The 1:1 ratio enhances the performance, allowing a puppeteer to incorporate single hand gestures without the complication of trying to manipulate both puppet hands along with the puppet mouth.

X-GRIP

Unless you were lucky enough to come with more than the two hands–two arms ratio standard of the usual human, you will find it a little difficult to manipulate both of your puppet's hands while simultaneously running the puppet's mouth. If you are the lone puppeteer working a puppet and can't rope a partner in for some close-contact tandem puppet working (hmmm, date night anyone?—ahem, I digress). . . . Basically, if you need an extra hand and don't have one available, the X-grip is your saving grace. This grip allows the puppeteer to work both puppet arms in the palm of one hand, which frees up the second hand for the puppet mouth.

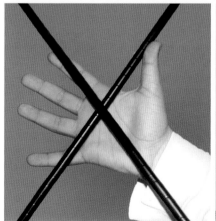

Basic position	Spread out	Drop to one rod	Back to two rods
	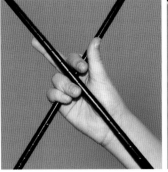		

ADVANCED GRIP

If continuing with puppets that need the use of both hands, and sometimes a pair of feet, the advanced grip is worth the time it takes to master. This is not an easy task to accomplish. These willful puppets are an active and vocal bunch, the demanding prima donnas of many a troupe. Thus, if you are not a Bunraku master working a three-humans-per-puppet ratio—ah, wouldn't that be a dream?—the necessity of manipulating both of the puppet hands with only one human hand, thus freeing that second human hand for either mouth or feet manipulation, will be a required skill.

NOW TRY THE FOLLOWING:

- Rub the puppet's head in confusion.
- Pat down his hair in nervous embarrassment.
- Hide his eyes from the audience by tucking his head into the crook of an elbow.
- Ponder thoughtfully with a finger/hand to the chin.
- Gesture an "aha" moment with an arm out in triumph.
- Keeping the hands still, have the puppet jump up and down an inch or so in excitement.
- Add a stage or platform, and now that you've got hands, try pulling the puppet up on stage. Start by peeking up over the edge of the platform. Look both ways—the coast is clear—now heave him the rest of the way up.

Constant use of arm rods is not a requirement. And just because they are there, it does not mean you have to be using them at all times. It is perfectly okay to let a hand controller drop free, still attached, until you are ready to pick it up again.

OOO-WAH! YAH!
WHAP. WAAAA,
KA-CHAH!
KARATE CHOP!

LOOK AT WHAT
I CAN DO.

"ALL THE WORLD'S A STAGE, AND ALL THE MEN AND WOMEN MERELY PLAYERS; THEY HAVE THEIR EXITS AND THEIR ENTRANCES, AND ONE MAN IN HIS TIME PLAYS MANY PARTS, HIS ACTS BEING SEVEN AGES. AT FIRST, THE INFANT, MEWLING AND PUKING IN THE NURSE'S ARMS. THEN THE WHINING SCHOOLBOY, WITH HIS ATCHEL AND SHINING MORNING FACE, CREEPING LIKE SNAIL UNWILLINGLY TO SCHOOL. AND THEN THE LOVER, SIGHING LIKE FURNACE, WITH A WOEFUL BALLAD O HIS MISTRESS' EYEBROW. DIER, FULL OF STRANGE ND BEARDED LIKE THE OUS IN HONOR, SUDDEN ICK IN QUARREL, SEEKING HE BUBBLE REPUTATION EVEN N THE CANNON'S MOUTH. AND JUSTICE, IN FAIR ROUND APON LINED, D BEARD F WISE ANCES; T. THE E LEAN , WITH POUCH OSE, WIDE HIS AIN PES LAST

chapter 4

BUILDING THE STAGE

TIME TO GO PRO

No longer satisfied with puppets alone? All built up and nowhere to perform? From the simplest constructions to a carpenter's dream, these stages will have you performing your art out in no time flat.

You can always create a simple on-the-spot stage by tying a rope between two trees and hanging a sheet over it clothesline style. The sheet screens the puppeteer from the audience's view, so this type of stage is often called a "screen." Consider taking it up a notch by painting a scene with inexpensive craft store acrylics for added ambiance. If you decide to go with a painted theme, consider a trip to your local library, where you can peruse a dozen or so picture books for superb design ideas. But if you want a little more stage variety, try your hand at the following examples.

SIMPLE SEWN STAGE

The easiest way to create a simple stage is to buy an opaque curtain that will fit the width of your preferred doorway. Barring that, if you want to get a little more creative, using an old (but clean) sheet is a great way to ease into the stage arena.

supplies

- Sewing machine and thread
- Tape measure
- Spring-style curtain rod
- Flat sheet or large (doorway-sized) curtain or piece of fabric

OPTIONAL:

- Acrylic paints
- Paintbrushes
- Pencil
- Picture book examples (fiction or nonfiction)

directions

1 Decide the height and width you want your screen to be. For this simple screen, you are aiming for play board height and a width slightly wider than your chosen door frame. Play board height is usually around waist height for an adult. You could also measure it as the height of an adult sitting on a chair plus enough added inches to cover the adult's head so that the audience doesn't see said adult.

NOT JUST FOR BEGINNERS

This type of painted screen can also be used for the intermediate and the advanced stages. It can be the in-front screen that keeps the puppeteer's lower half hidden from the audience, or it can be the upper backdrop screen that a puppet plays against, much like a stage set for a play. If you already have a stage frame, use that as your measuring guide. Measure and mark the sheet accordingly.

With care, these painted works can last for years, but do expect a little bit of crackling and wear to show through prolonged folding and use.

2 Cut sheet or fabric down to size, leaving room for the rod pocket, the side hems, and the bottom hem.

3 Sew the top hem, leaving enough room to run the spring rod through.

4 Sew the side hems, if needed, and then sew the bottom hem.

5 If you decide to paint your curtain, sketch out the design outline in chalk or pencil first. Then move on to Step 6. If you will not be painting the sheet, then you are done. Run the spring rod—the tension rod—through the pocket, and hang it in the doorway or string it between those trees.

6 Start painting. Work from left to right if you are a righty and right to left for you lefties. This helps in the anti-smear department by allowing you to move away from fresh paint into new areas without dragging your arm across the scene. Let the last of the paint dry, string up your creation, and let the fun begin.

Not only is this an ideal quick-up, quick-down stage, it's compact, lightweight, and easy to transport to and from not only the babysitting job but also grandma and grandpa's house.

OPTION:

Add a second spring rod with attached dark (black or dark blue) tricot fabric for an upper screen as a stand-up option. With a tricot screen hanging at the top of the doorway—down to a point a few inches below the top of the first opaque and/or painted screen—a puppeteer can stand up. Just duck the puppets under the tricot and let them "play" at play board level above the bottom screen. Make sure the puppeteer's side of the room is dark, with lights on in the audience arena. This allows the puppeteer to see out without audience being able to see in. Tricot fabric is kind of great that way.

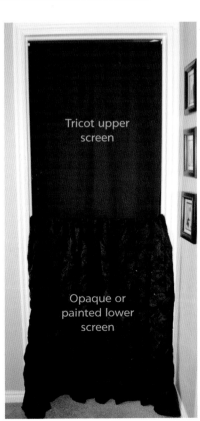

Tricot upper screen

Opaque or painted lower screen

Front view of stage

INTERMEDIATE PVC PIPE STAGE

This PVC pipe stage is fairly inexpensive while maintaining a relatively easy-up, easy-down setup—all while still being sturdy and transportable.

I won't kid you; disassembling and reassembling a complicated PVC stage can test the restraint of most human beings on the planet. Preplanning, color-coding, and/or clear labeling will go a long way toward making the job easier.

supplies

- Sewing machine and thread
- PVC pipe cutters or hacksaw with a serrated blade
- Electrical or masking tape
- PVC pipe 1 inch to 1 1/4 inches in diameter, cut into the lengths listed in Step 1
- Four PVC pipe elbow connectors that fit the diameter of your pipe
- Four PVC pipe 3-way connectors that fit the diameter of your pipe
- Two PVC pipe caps that fit the diameter of your pipe (optional)
- Tricot fabric or other partially transparent, dark-colored fabric, about 6 feet wide by 3 feet tall
- Opaque fabric or curtain*, about 6 feet wide by about 4–5 feet tall

OPTIONAL SIDE CURTAINS:

- Opaque fabric or curtain, about 6–7 feet wide by about 4 1/2–5 feet tall
- Hook-and-loop tape, about 1–2 feet

directions

1 Cut PVC pipe with a hacksaw or PVC pipe cutters—or nicely ask the handy home improvement store associate to cut the PVC pipe—in the following measurements:

- Four pieces of pipe 12 inches (1 foot) each—for horizontal floor supports
- Two pieces of pipe 24 inches (2 feet) each—for middle horizontal floor supports
- Two pieces of pipe 42 inches (3 1/2 feet) each—for front uprights
- Two pieces of pipe 66 inches (5 1/2 feet) each—for front and back horizontals
- Two more pieces of pipe 66 inches (5 1/2 feet) each—for back uprights

The length of the middle pieces can be varied according to your personal tastes. Adjust any side curtains accordingly.

FABRIC TIP

*Opaque decorative fabric shower curtains make excellent front screens, as they wear well and shed most dirt and scuff marks easily.

CUTTING PVC

Mark the PVC cuts by wrapping masking or electrical tape around the pipe. This is a great visual that assists in keeping the cuts straight.

"WHEN WE ARE BORN, WE CRY THAT WE ARE COME TO THIS GREAT STAGE OF FOOLS."

THE TRICOT TRICK

Tricot is an inexpensive fabric that allows a puppeteer, sitting in the dark of the backstage area, to still be able to see an audience that is in a lighted room. Feel free to test other fabric blends, particularly if they are on sale. Look for deals on semitransparent (and often stretchy) Lycra®/polyester blends for a non-wrinkling curtain, or even use 100 percent polyester black or dark-colored suiting fabrics.

Back view of stage without side curtains

2 Now you will connect the floor base assembly. Make two sets. Each horizontal (flat on the floor) floor base is composed of the three shortest pipes with two 3-way connectors between them, in this order: pipe/3-way connector/longer pipe/3-way connector/pipe. The optional caps will go on the pipes that face the audience.

3 Slide a front upright (the 3 1/2 foot–sized PVC—the shorter of the two uprights) into the upward-facing opening in one of the 3-way connectors in the floor base assembly. Repeat for the other floor base.

4 Top the two front uprights with two elbow connectors. Spread the two floor assemblies about 5 feet apart.

5 Insert the first 5-foot horizontal pipe into the elbows of those front uprights. Your assembly should stand on its own now.

THINK AHEAD

The height of the stage is adjustable and should be based on the prospective puppeteer's size. The size also depends on how you plan to use your stage (e.g., if you prefer a stage that allows a puppeteer to sit on a chair instead of kneel, or maybe you are making a child-sized stage).

EXTRA FABRIC?

Leftover pieces of tricot are excellent easy-on, easy-off linings to use on the inside of your puppets, a particularly useful attribute when puppeteering through several quick-change puppet transitions.

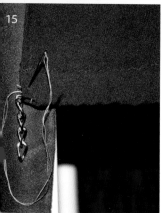

6 Slide each of the two 6-foot uprights (the tall ones) into the upward-facing opening of the remaining back 3-way connectors of the floor bases.

7 Top these two tallest uprights with two elbow connectors.

8 Insert the last 5-foot horizontal pipe into the upper elbow connectors.

9 Measure how high the play board section of the stage is, just to make sure. The play board is where all the action happens, and it's the front horizontal pipe. Measure how wide the play board section is, as well. This measurement will be the final size of the bottom or front screen curtain, the one that screens a sitting or kneeling puppeteer from the audience.

10 Sew a 3- to 5-inch pocket in the top of the curtain or opaque fabric, testing the fit of the pipe in the pocket, as the size of the pocket needed will depend on the size of the PVC pipe. You want the front horizontal pipe to fit nicely through this pocket, this is the pipe that your curtain will hang from. Run the front horizontal pipe through the newly sewn pocket and reinsert the now curtain-laden front pipe back into the elbow connectors. This way, you can accurately measure the length from the top to the bottom hem. Pin the hem while hanging for the best fit. A little extra length is always a good idea to ensure no accidental puppeteer exposure happens. Extra length is also useful when sandbags are needed in gusty outdoor conditions.

11 Remove the curtain from the pipe and sew the bottom hem according to your measurement in Step 10. Consider sewing a small-rolled hem* on each of the sides of the curtain for a nice finished look. If you are using a pre-finished curtain or adding the optional side curtains, the rolled hems will not be needed.

*Small-rolled hems are a snap to sew if you already know how. New to sewing? See page 143 in the Resources section.

12 It's time to test fit the top—the upper screen—curtain and measure the hem placement. Sew a 3- to 5-inch pocket in the tricot or partially transparent fabric. This is a repeat of what you did with the opaque front screen in Step 10. Run the pipe through the newly sewn pocket and hang the upper horizontal pipe back up.

13 With your upper horizontal pipe in place, measure from the top of the pipe to the top of the front screen curtain. Add approximately 5 inches to your measurement. The extra inches give you room for the bottom hem and a little extra for ensuring the puppeteer stays hidden. The goal is to cover the puppeteer but to not be an annoyance when puppets enter and perform.

14 Finish off the two side seams with a small-rolled hem. Then sew a 1- to 2-inch bottom hem based on your measurements from Step 13.

15 Run a small- to mid-sized chain through the bottom hem. Hand sew the ends of the chain into the pocket to prevent accidental slippage and loss of chain. This weighted top screen is a puppeteer's best friend, as it keeps the lightweight top screen fabric from

catching on a puppet as he or she attempts to enter or walk along the stage.

That's it! You've created, assembled, and curtained a thoroughly workable PVC pipe stage. Give yourself a congratulatory high five. Sit back and marvel at your creation. But wait; are you visualizing your prospective venues? Are you going to fill those audience seats to the max? Maybe some optional side curtains to block the back-of-the-stage view from those extended audience sizes are in order.

optional side curtains

1 Measure the side space between the front and back uprights. If you used 2-foot floor spacers, it should be 2 feet wide. The height will be the same as your bottom curtain from Step 9 in the Intermediate PVC Pipe Stage instructions. This will be the finished measurement you are aiming for in your side curtains.

2 Cut the curtain or opaque fabric down to size, leaving room for three small-rolled hems and the to-the-front-screen seam.

3 Sew the front edge of each side curtain to its respective side edge of the front screen. Carefully pin the rod pocket openings well away from the sewing machine's path. You don't want to block off the rod pockets.

4 Finish the other three raw edges of the cut curtain by sewing small-rolled seams.

5 Now you'll attach the side curtains to the back uprights. Cut two strips of the loop side (the soft side) of some hook-and-loop tape, making sure each piece of tape fits nicely around the pipes with about a 1/2-inch to 1-inch overlap. Measure the height of the front curtain and mark the measurement on the back PVC uprights. Using your strongest adhesive, glue the hook-and-loop tape around the back uprights over the top of your marked height measurements. Let adhesive dry thoroughly.

6 Sew the remaining two hook-and-loop tape pieces (it's only the hook side; you've already used the fuzzy loop side on the pipes) to the upper back edge of the

Tricot upper curtain

Side curtain

Opaque lower curtain

Stage with side curtains

FOR THE MEASUREMENT CHALLENGED

Yes, I sewed the hems after attaching the two curtains. But then, I don't trust my fabric measuring skills very much. If you can easily visualize what sewing needs to be done where, and you trust your measurements, go ahead and sew the hems first and then the seam to attach the side curtains to the front curtain.

Attached side curtains

side curtains like a dog's tail. This piece will wrap around the upright with the companion piece of hook-and-loop tape to hold the curtain up and in place. Add a few more of these wrapped holders in the middle and the bottom of the side curtains if you plan on performing outdoors where wind issues can arise.

There. Done. Now you can relax. Good job! Well, almost. Kind of. If you really want to be done, you can be. But if you are a perfectionist, there's just a bit more. Is the bright white of PVC pipe not blending well with your curtains? Consider painting the PVC pipes at this point, but do take note that the only PVC that needs painting is the visible part. It's a good idea to paint all the uprights and the floor assembly, but spare yourself the trouble of painting anything near the ends of the horizontal pipes; they'll be covered with the curtains, and you do not want any issues with sliding any interchangeable screens over painted pipes. Now that wasn't so bad, was it?

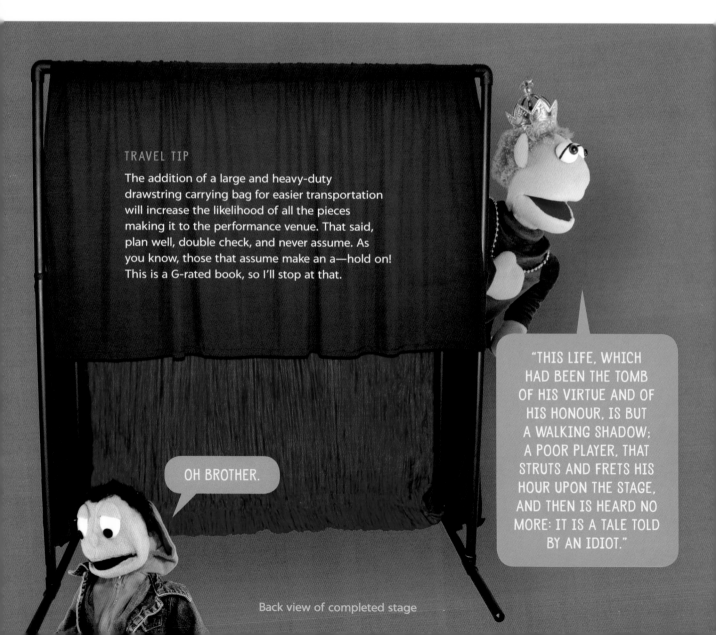

TRAVEL TIP

The addition of a large and heavy-duty drawstring carrying bag for easier transportation will increase the likelihood of all the pieces making it to the performance venue. That said, plan well, double check, and never assume. As you know, those that assume make an a—hold on! This is a G-rated book, so I'll stop at that.

OH BROTHER.

"THIS LIFE, WHICH HAD BEEN THE TOMB OF HIS VIRTUE AND OF HIS HONOUR, IS BUT A WALKING SHADOW; A POOR PLAYER, THAT STRUTS AND FRETS HIS HOUR UPON THE STAGE, AND THEN IS HEARD NO MORE: IT IS A TALE TOLD BY AN IDIOT."

Back view of completed stage

a one-size-fits-all method

If assembling and disassembling the PVC stage puts you in a sweat before and after each show, consider using what we learned (and have permission to share) from our friends in the Maxed-Out-Puppet Troupe. They developed a one-size-fits-all construction method:

- Cut all vertical PVC pipes 4 feet long.
- Cut all horizontal PVC pipes 6 feet long.
- Build up (the vertical pipes) with 2-way PVC pipe connectors.
- Build out (horizontally) with 3-way connectors that allow you to branch out into the curtain-holding pipes.
- Lay down floor supports in the 4-foot size.

(Google them for some great puppetry hijinks and fun.)

ADVANCED WOODEN STAGE

Nothing beats a professional-grade plywood, sheeting wood, or Masonite® puppet stage. And if you make it so that it disassembles and folds for easier transportation, you won't regret the effort put into it.

Durable and easy to set up, this stage almost makes up for the fact that it is large (small car = no go) and heavier than the doorway or PVC stages.

WOODEN GATE-FOLD STAGE

supplies

- Table saw
- Hammer
- Power drill with accompanying wood drill and screw bits to match both the sizing and the heads of your chosen screws
- Pliers
- Pencil
- PVC pipe cutters
- Sewing machine and thread
- Skinny nail to hammer in pilot holes (although I highly recommend using the power drill with a small drill bit)
- Assorted paintbrushes (optional)
- One sheet of standard 48-inch-by-96-inch plywood, Masonite®, or other sturdy board of choice, 1/2–3/4 inch thick, cut into measurements found in Steps 1–3

NOTE:

Standard door hinges are a cheap and readily available hinge option; just plan on devising an attachment method for the removable nail/pin, as it is easy to lose. We suggest a chain or string that attaches directly from the pin to the hinge or stage. We still worry about losing those nails—make sure you have a few extra in your Performance Emergency Kit found in the Resources section on page 145.

CUTTING PLYWOOD

If you are particularly nice, you can often make full use of your local home improvement store's customer service policy that allows for free cutting and have the super friendly store associates cut your plywood in the sizes you need before you even leave the store.

- One 3-foot piano hinge (sometimes referred to as a continuous hinge) with 1/2 inch–long flathead wood screws to fit the hinge holes (we used #6-sized wood screws). Each continuous hinge will have a different quantity of holes for the screws, depending on how long of a hinge you purchase. Since you are discarding the too-long screws that come with the hinge, make sure you count how many of the shorter 1/2-inch screws you will need.
- Four door hinges and four large nails to replace the larger and harder-to-remove hinge pins or, if you can find them, two heavy-duty right hand lift-off cabinet hinges and two heavy-duty left hand lift-off hinges (e.g., the Fastenal® 40S Aluminum Economy Liftoff Hinge), with 1/2-inch flathead wood screws to fit the hinge holes
- Six 40-inch long pieces of 3/4-inch PVC pipe
- Twenty-four 3/4-inch galvanized pipe straps
- Twenty-four 1 1/4 inch–long flathead #8 machine bolts and matching wing nuts (or standard nuts)
- Twelve scraps of 1-inch-by-1-inch wood blocks
- Two galvanized hook-and-eye latches
- Ample quantity of 1/2-, 3/4-, and 1-inch #6 and #8 flathead wood screws
- Tricot fabric, at least 144 inches (12 feet) by 48 inches (4 feet)
- Two 23-inch curtain rods with 1/2 inch–long wood screws to fit the curtain rod holes
- One 50-inch curtain rod with 1/2 inch–long wood screws to fit the curtain rod holes
- Metal chain, small to mid-sized (for weighting tricot curtains)

OPTIONAL:

- Wood glue (for securing wood screws when working with the more fragile plywood base)
- Spray and/or standard paints

A HELPFUL GUIDE FOR CUTTING PLYWOOD

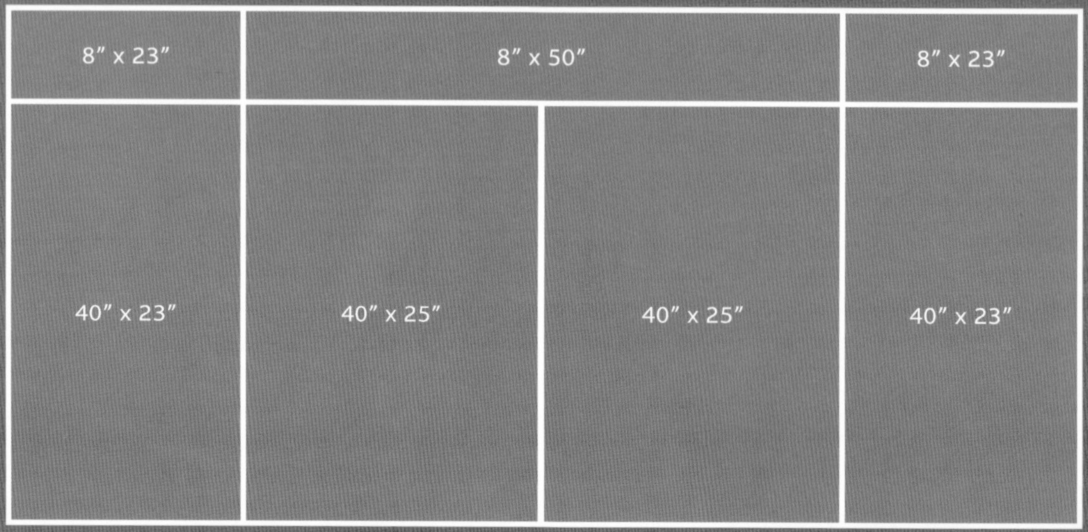

8" x 23"	8" x 50"		8" x 23"
40" x 23"	40" x 25"	40" x 25"	40" x 23"

directions

1 Using the sheet of standard 48-inch-tall-by-96 inch-wide 1/2- to 3/4-inch plywood, cut plywood sheet down from 48 inches tall to 40 inches tall (refer to diagram on opposite page). Save the remaining 8 inches for the next step: the sign board banner.

2 Cut the 8-inch-by-96-inch sign board banner into one 50 inch–long segment and two 23 inch–long segments. This gives you one 8-inch-by-50-inch piece and two 8-inch-by-23-inch pieces. These are the top banners for the stage, the center piece (50 inches) and two wings (23 inches each).

3 Cut the 40 inch–wide plywood down from 96 inches wide into two 23-inch sections (the wings) and two 25-inch pieces (the centers). These pieces will become the main front piece and wings of the stage.

4 Cut the PVC pipes into six lengths, each 40 inches tall. These are the banner board–holding uprights. Use the PVC pipe cutters or a hacksaw.

5 Place the piano hinge on the front (audience side) of the two 25-inch stage base pieces. Attach the hinge along the 40-inch sides. Drop the hinge down from what will be the top of the stage no more than 4–6 inches. It's better to have a larger non-hinged gap at the bottom than the top for durability. Pushing the two 25-inch fronts as tightly together as possible, mark the screw holes on the plywood.

6 With a slightly smaller-gauge drill bit than your screws, drill pilot holes in all the marked locations.

7 Using your pilot holes as a guide, screw and attach the piano hinge to the 25-inch wood bases. Remember: do not use the pre-packaged screws that came with the hinge; they will be too long and the sharp tips will extend through to the back of most any still-light-enough-to-easily-transport plywood. And I probably don't need to tell you that the back of a puppet stage (the place where the puppeteer's exposed arms and a puppet's tender skin are most likely to come in excruciating contact with said sharp, pokey bits) is not the place for screws and nails to be exposed and protruding.

8 Attach the two side wings with the four door hinges or the lift-off hinges. One half of each hinge attaches to the center base, and the other half attaches to its matching wing. Make sure your hinges open and close in the correct direction—the wings need to wrap around to the back side of the stage. Measure, mark, and drill pilot holes before screwing the hinges in. Remember: the screws that come in any pre-packaged hinge set will be too long. 1/2 inch–long #8 flathead wood screws are just about perfect for 3/4-inch plywood—two hinges per side, each about 4–6 inches from the top or bottom edge, respectively.

CUTTING PVC

Home improvement store associates are usually very helpful in the PVC cutting department as well.

IMPORTANT!

Double check and make sure the hinge is positioned to fold the two front pieces together toward the front (that's still the audience side). If you screw the hinge on backwards, the stage will not fold. The center is designed to fold flat, protecting any audience-facing paint creation, not to mention that the hardware you will be placing on the back of the stage will prevent the hinge from folding flat in the back—the resulting pressure would pop that piano hinge right out of the wood.

MAKE IT LAST

The hinge is likely to be exposed to a lot of torque (twisting pressure) during transportation; the addition of some strong wood glue will extend the life of your stage.

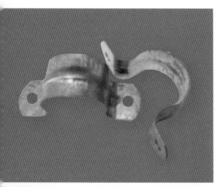

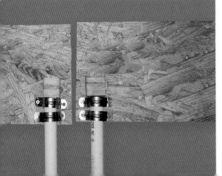

9 Before screwing the pipe straps in, you will want to stretch the straps out a bit to ease in disassembling the stage for porting it around. Use the pliers to open them up a bit as shown in the illustration. This stretching is not necessary if your stage will have a permanent home.

10 Turn the stage over so that the piano hinge is no longer visible. You will be working on the back of the stage now. Place the header boards flush against the top edge of the fully assembled and hinged base—just as if you had never cut off 8 inch–tall header boards—in order to line up pipe strap locations on both the base and the headers. You will be attaching two pipe straps for each PVC pipe's end. (That's four straps per pipe: two on the bottom and two on the top header.) You will use two PVC pipes, one on each side of each of the wings. The remaining two PVC pipes will attach on each side of the center (piano-hinged portion) of the base.

11 Place the straps 1 inch down from the play area edges (that's 1 inch down from the play board edge of the bottom base but 1 inch up from the bottom of the headers) of the boards with the strap flanges flush with the sides. Again, mark and drill pilot holes—but only drill on ONE side of each strap. The other side of the straps will be bolted in Step 12. Attach straps with 1/2-inch #8 screws in those pre-drilled holes. Repeat for each of the twenty-four straps.

12 The other sides of the straps will be bolted instead of screwed. Place the drill bit in each of the open (not screwed in) pipe strap holes—do I need to add that you only do this one at a time? I don't think so; you're smart enough to have made it this far and I think you can handle it—and drill a hole completely through the stage from the back to the front. Repeat for all twenty-four straps—bases and headers. You are now ready to stand the stage up.

13 From the front of the stage—going in through the front—drive each machine screw through the back and into each of the drilled pipe strap holes. Use the 1 1/4-inch #8 flathead machine bolts. Do not tighten down with the nuts yet. Insert PVC pipes into the pipe straps (pushing the headers up and thus opening up the "play space" of the stage). Now add the wing nuts to the ends of the bolts and tighten the straps over the PVC pipes. Pliers make handy wing nut tighteners.

14 Mark and pre-drill pilot holes and then screw in hook-and-eye latches between the two wing headers and the center header. When measuring placement, remember to leave room for your curtain rods and for the wings to fold in and back on the puppeteer. That said, you will want a nice tight fit to eliminate any header wobbles. This step can be done with the stage upright and the wings bent in to best make sure your placement is perfect. But some laying down of the stage to actually drill and screw in the hooks might be necessary for those of us who have a height disadvantage.

15 Screw curtain rods, centered, to the back of the headers—the long 50-inch rod to the middle header and the two 23-inch rods to the wing headers. Again, do not use the pre-packaged hardware. Use the shorter 1/2-inch #8, or #6 if the holes are smaller, flathead wood screws.

16 If you've laid the stage down and have been working on a flat surface at this point, go ahead and stand the stage upright.

17 Measure the distance between the curtain rods and the play board (top of the base). Add about 5 inches. Make sure you have enough room to sew a pocket for the curtain rods to slide through and a bottom hem with a bit extra at the bottom for complete puppeteer coverage.

18 Cut the curtain fabric—72 inches wide and about 48 inches tall for the center, and 36 inches wide and 48 inches tall for each wing.

19 Sew the rod pockets. Hang curtains on the rods to re-measure and mark the hem lines.

20 Remove the curtains and finish off each of the two sides with small-rolled hems. Then sew the bottom hems, leaving a 1- to 2-inch pocket to run the weighting chain through.

21 Run the weighted chain through the bottom hems, then hand stitch a few chain links near each opening and end to keep the chain in place and secure.

OPTION:

If you really don't want to mess with accidental loss of curtain, omit the curtain rods and secure those curtains directly to the wood. Use your imagination and creativity and I'm sure you'll come up with a solution that works for you, from hook-and-loop tape to the judicious placement of grommets, optional washers, and screws.

HEAVY DUTY DOES IT

If you are an energetic puppeteer—and let's face it, most of us are—consider using good, strong curtain rods, not full home-building-stand-up-against-a-curtain-pulling-toddler-sized rods, but strong enough to sturdily and securely attach to the header.

SERIOUSLY? TWENTY-ONE STEPS? WHO WROTE THIS, ANYWAY?

FABRIC TIPS:

For a less permanent fabric solution: sew a fabric cover and, instead of using adhesives and nails or screws, use elastic straps—looped around and secured to the back with hooks—for an inter-changeable front.

Additionally, if you fre-quent secondhand shops that carry home goods, a good brocade 96-inch-by-40-inch curtain is just about perfect for this stage. Better yet—the edges are already neatly hemmed and finished for you. Just add the heavy-duty elastic straps, four straps per side for eight total. This option usually necessitates the addition of painting the top and bottom edges of your stage, as it is a tight stretch and a bit of expo-sure is bound to happen. But then it's a good idea to heavily paint plywood edges anyway—it will result in an easier grip, fewer splinters, and lon-ger-lasting wood overall.

FINAL TOUCHES

Hang the curtains back up and you are in the home stretch! Let's finish this stage with the final touches. It's time to get your creative on. Let's paint and get this stage perfectified and performance ready! Choose your style:

option one: paint-free stage

Not into painting all that bumpy, lumpy, not-so-smooth plywood? Cover the plywood pieces with fabric. Just wrap fabric up and over the edges, and hold it in place with spray glue. Using short flathead nails, nail the fabric edges in place. Cover the center separately from the wings. Remember, the wings detach; your fabric covering should too.

For the PVC, sew up some fabric tubes, or follow the non-sew method of using spray adhesive and just wrap the fabric around the pipes. Remember to only cover the portions of the pipes that the audience can see; you need to leave room for the pipes to slip in and out of the pipe straps.

option two: painted stage

Let your inner artist out, allow the creative juices to run free (just don't drip on any wet paint), and start decorating this baby up. Grab the paints and brushes and paint the front of the plywood, the banner pieces, and the PVC uprights until every bit of the audience-facing stage is covered and is as prettified as desired. Use a good plastic-adhering spray paint, preferably in a curtain-matching black, for the PVC.

A FEW MORE TIPS

when assembling and disassembling the wooden gate-fold stage:

1 Stand upright and open the front two (piano-hinged) pieces in an open V shape. Slip each of the wings onto their respective hinges. Your stage footprint now resembles a wide-open M.

2 Bend the wings around toward the puppeteer and the back of the stage. Flatten out the center of the stage. As you finish, the front will be flat and the wings will be at not-quite-90-degree angles from the front.

3 Slide the PVC uprights into the header pipe straps. Slip the banner board–laden PVC uprights into the pipe straps on the stage base. Tighten all wing nuts or bolts. (Hmm, I wonder if there is such a thing as a wing nut tightener? If not, those pliers are very handy.)

4 If curtains aren't permanently attached to the headers, hang the curtain-laden curtain rods on the banner boards. Curtains can easily be rolled up for transportation with no need to remove them from the rods.

5 Slip the two banner anti-wobble hooks into their respective eyes.

6 Just reverse the steps above to disassemble. But then, I don't think I needed to tell you that. You're a right smart bunch to have purchased this book in the first place, after all.

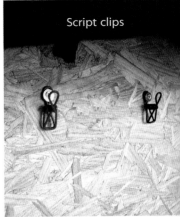

Script clips

additional suggestions:

- Are you a script-reading puppeteer? Add script-holding clips to the back of the stage with screws and washers.
- If you've still got some spray paint, preferably in two different and distinct colors, consider adding the quick-see visual of a shape that lines up the front and the wings. This way, you'll never get them upside down or on the wrong side.

Paint some set-up guides

DON'T FORGET TO PACK YOUR EMERGENCY KIT

When performing for a traveling show, particularly one with a wooden stage, be sure to visit the Resources section for information on packing a puppeteer's Traveling Emergency Supply Kit.

ONE CAVEAT WITH THIS STAGE:

Don't get overly excited mid-puppet show! Any undue forward pressure will push the stage over flat in—you guessed it—no time flat. You can add optional footers or bases by creating a set of grooved feet that the plywood front can slip into, or you could attach a flat "floor" for the puppeteer to sit on. Use your ingenuity—it comes naturally to us puppeteers.

- How about adding rings or heavy-duty alligator clips to the back to hold your in-the-wings-and-waiting-for-their-turn puppets ready and upside down to easily slip onto busy puppeteer hands?
- If you aren't using over-the-ear microphones for your sound system, add a holder for a microphone.
- While you are at it, if you plan on having electricity, add another holder for a small light to shine on your hanging script.
- And—okay, one last thing—if you don't use a paper script and are a more tech-oriented puppeteer, consider adding a holder for a tablet. The need for a backstage helper will be required for this, as even touch tablets need a free finger (noses will work in a pinch, but aren't recommended) to scroll the script forward.

Now you can truly sit back and take a deep breath. Phew. That was a big job. Go get some ice cream to reward yourself for sticking to it. It might also be a good reward for your loved ones who have maybe had an earful of some of the more frustrating and even painful moments that are an unfortunate side product inherent in the non-professional wood worker and stage builder's apprenticeship. We all know that the family that plays together stays together, but sometimes getting to the "play" part requires patience and understanding liberally sprinkled with "I'm sorry" and reciprocated with many an "I may not fully understand, but I still love you."

AND REMEMBER: NO MATTER HOW FRUSTRATING IT GETS, NO FOWL LANGUAGE, OKAY?

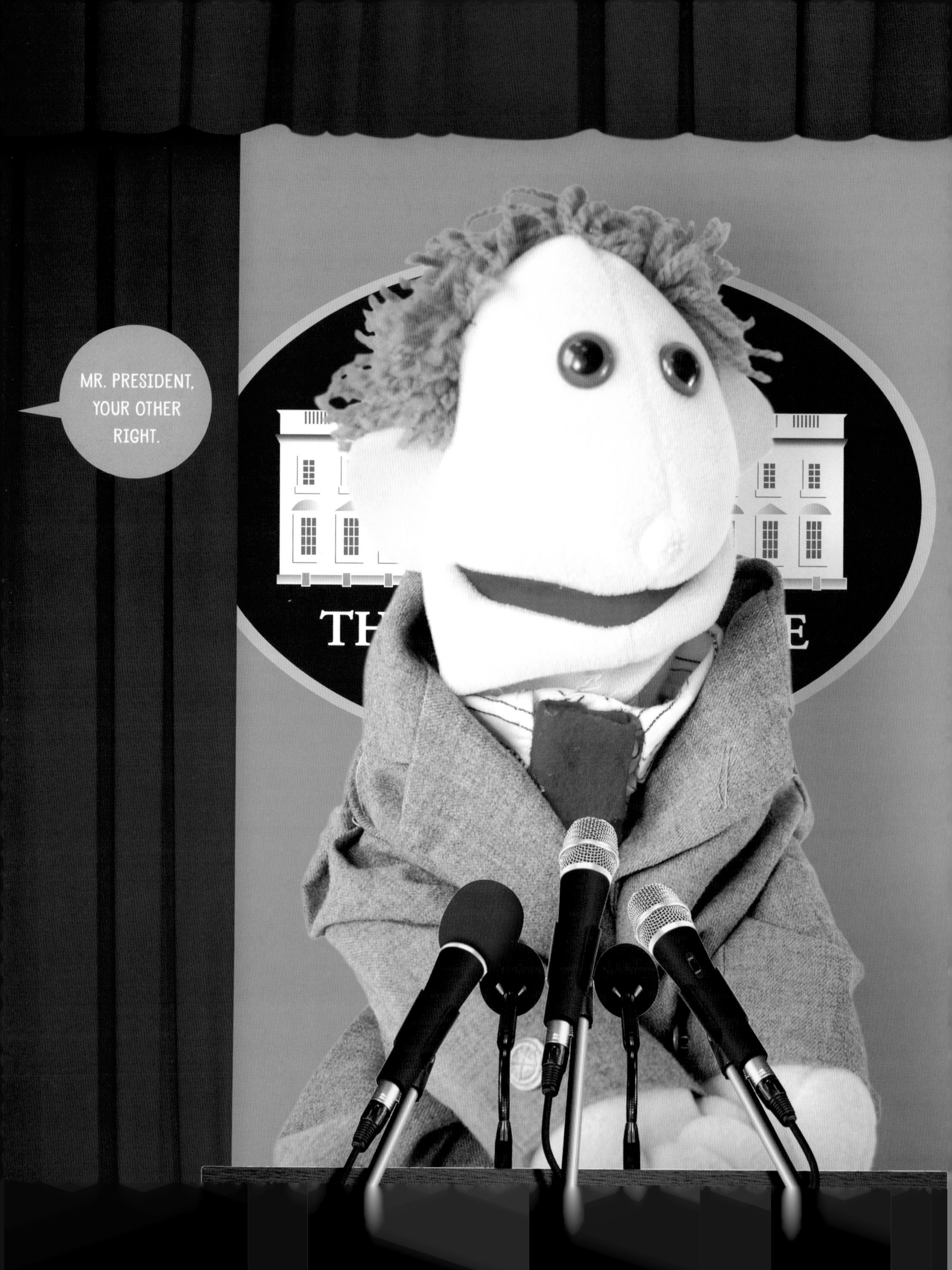
MR. PRESIDENT, YOUR OTHER RIGHT.

PART II

ACTING LESSONS

MASTERING THE ART OF PERFORMANCE

chapter 5

BODY LANGUAGE & EMOTION

REALLY, HIGGINS, YOU NEED TO FIND ANOTHER HOBBY. EVER TRY GROWING PETUNIAS?

FOLLOW ALONG WITH MARK IN

"MY FAIR PUPPET"

FEELING THE POWER OF SILENT FILM

Let's hit the boards, peop—I mean, puppets!

Before the "talkies" and the subsequent demise of the silent film star (we won't go into the tragic story of Rin Tin Tin here), there was only body language to get the message across. Now it's your turn to practice the silent art of the body wherein you and your puppet can speak volumes without saying a single word.

WARM UP AND PREP

Loosen up those joints and strengthen those shoulders! Arms up. Puppets on. Are we set?

Oh, and, upon occasion, remember to "get blood," that is, drop your arms and shake some blood flow into those famished fingers.

LOOK DOWN

Note your audience's location. If you are on a raised platform, you will need to tip your puppet's head down even further. The same is true if your puppet's eyes are on the top of his head.

EYE CONTACT

WATCH FUN EXAMPLES IN "MY FAIR PUPPET" VIDEO #2

Maintaining proper eye contact is crucial in any conversation; puppets are no exception to the rule. Watch your puppet closely; if he's looking off in the distance or, worse, has his eyes on the ceiling, your audience will naturally follow his gaze. Before you can say "Jack Sprat" (the one with no fat), you will have lost your audience's attention.

So buckle down. Get busy. It's time to get your head out of the clouds and look the audience in the eye . . . unless the puppet is daydreaming, looking skyward in feigned innocence, or possibly reminiscing about something in the past, of course.

The audience needs to see the puppet's eyes in order to be able to interpret expressions and attitudes. A slight bend forward will do the trick.

HEAD BOBBING

WATCH FUN EXAMPLES IN "MY FAIR PUPPET" VIDEO #3

Bob and weave, mate. Bob and weave. As you move, so does your head. Watch as people walk. Does that person have a bit of a side-to-side movement to his or her walk? How about adding a bit of bounce in there? It's not hard to do, once you get the idea. As with many things in life, half the battle is in the knowing.

Slow, fast, a calculated look to the left, a quick take to the right: head movement is all attitude and timing. Mesmerize the audience with this move: tilt the head slightly down, and scan the audience from one side to the next. Stop. Focus on one person. Continue the scan. Do a little double take to another idle audience member. Remember: the audience will follow the puppet's gaze. Test it out. It's quite possible to get a few belly laughs out of this little trick. Don't overdo it, though. You don't have to look every audience member in the eye; just a few will do. Less is more.

A HINT FROM HIGGINS: DON'T OVERDO IT

Do be careful: unnecessary nodding will get you nowhere. Don't nod if you've got nothing to say. Instead of a constant head bob to indicate your puppet is really and truly paying attention, you can let the puppet's mouth hang slightly open.

ANOTHER HINT FROM HIGGINS: WALK, DON'T FLOAT

Walking is much different than floating; it's a difference you can see. If your puppet smoothly moves across the stage without any up-and-down motion, it will look like your puppet is mysteriously gliding on a sheet of ice . . . which is fine, if that's what he is doing. But if your puppet is walking from one place to the next, you're going to have to show that with a bit more movement.

practice

Picture a happy-go-lucky bloke and his brand of head movements. They won't be the same as the ones you get from a nose-in-the-air society gal or, for that matter, a monster on the prowl. Get into character and let individual puppet personality shine through.

THE BODY IN MOTION

WATCH FUN EXAMPLES IN "MY FAIR PUPPET" VIDEO #3

Take a hike. Stop to catch your breath. Lean in to hear a secret. Flop in despair. From simple to extreme, a puppet's body language can speak volumes before the puppet utters his first syllable.

Again, be careful. More is not always better, and while movement is essential, there is a fine line between too much and too little.

Now one, two, three . . .

practice time

- Let's take an elevator ride. "Ding. Ninth floor, ladies' shoes . . . "
- Escalator? Up. Down.
- Can you imitate using a cane to walk? How about a demonstrating a guffaw-inducing stumble? Can you do the hokey pokey? Practice and have fun, 'cause after all, that's what it's all about.
- Want some more practice? Put on some of your favorite music and get your groove on. Dance up a storm. Put on the moves. Too much too soon? Terrified of looking a fool? Don't sweat it! Practice in front of your mirror with just you, yourself, and your puppet, and rock on. You might want to close your bedroom door first or wait until you are alone in the house.

POSTURE TAKES PRACTICE . . . LOTS OF PRACTICE

Good puppet posture takes practice. Bad posture, or what is commonly called the "unintentional leaning puppet," is all too easy to do. It's keeping your arm at an uncomfortable 90-degree angle that is unnatural. Practice is the key to holding the correct positioning for long periods of time.

CONVEYING EMOTION

WATCH FUN EXAMPLES IN "MY FAIR PUPPET" VIDEO #6

Put it all together at last, from the drop-dead hilarious to the melodramatic tragedy. Sighing, sleeping, crying, concern, confusion, sadness, fear, excitement: we do it all naturally. The trick is to have your puppet imitate what you already do. If in doubt, overemphasize the emotions. Dramatic moods require dramatic moves. The key to believability is staying in character. No flopping, stopping, or otherwise sloppy puppeteering for you!

scared

Are you feeling a little tense? Got the midnight jitters? Are you ripe for a good fright? It's the shivering and shaking that convey the message here. But be careful: while constant shaking might do the trick, you can create a more realistic experience if you allow your puppet to tremble in fits and starts.

excited

Are you the antsy type? Feeling a bit perky or maybe a little bouncy? In any case, your puppet can exhibit these emotions with a bit of up-and-down, ants-in-the-pants action. Imagine that you've just been given the best gift ever or that you are not-so-patiently waiting for a surprise. What would you be doing? Careful now, restrain a little of that enthusiasm; dancing isn't going to make time go any faster.

surprised

It's all about doing the double take. "Is that a monster in my house?" Surprise! Whether it's a jaw dropper, a head shaker, or a moment of disbelief, pause for a moment of confusion followed by a sudden jolting start. Getting in a good surprise is loads of fun. Got it down? Take time to enjoy the moment before taking it further. Go slow. Go quick. Once, twice; it's up to you—gauge how much your audience is enjoying it. Follow up with an open-mouthed squealing squeak before dashing off the stage!

confused

Tip your head as if you are listening closely. A slow opening of the mouth . . . is it the "oh" of dawning understanding? Maybe a head tilt to the other side. Scratch your head, if you've got hands. The ultimate "I give up" shoulder shrug and walk away is a classic example of confusion, or you can try the slow-on-the-uptake "Just give me a minute; I know I'll get it. Eventually . . . "

concerned

Give a bit of a headshake—slow and deliberate, from side to side—a slight nod in sympathetic understanding, or even a commiserating pat on the back in sympathy if there's more than one character on stage.

understanding

Light bulb! Slowly let the bottom jaw drop into an open-mouthed look of surprise; accompany it with a slow head turn back to the source of the inspiration, whether it be a fellow puppet, a vocal audience member, or even the puppeteer.

distraught

Flop over onto your back. Mouth open, bemoan the fates and the unjustness of life in general. Ham it up and drag it out. Flop back to your front in despair; hang over the edge of the stage. There you go. You're on a roll! Milk it for all it's worth, baby!

Alternately, take a heavy sigh. Draw back your arm and add a slight lift of the shoulders, as if you're taking a deep breath. Now act it out: "Oh dear, oh dear, oh dear. I'm heartbroken and blue, blue as can be. Just let me mope and drag my heavy self around a bit."

If you're ready for it, add the illusion of tears. "No, no, no." Heave the shoulders, drop the head, and cry. "Waaaaahhh!" If you've got arms, rub those eyes like the babies on the bus. Wah, wah, wah!

angry

Stomp, huff, and make an angry face, i.e., that tightly closed mouth that says, "I'm irritated. I'm upset and a little bit miffed." Stiffen that neck; fix that directed gaze. Just don't aim those dangerous laser eyes in my direction.

sympathetic

"There, there." With a pat on the back, lean toward the puppet in need of sympathy. My oh my, what a kind, warm-hearted, and loving little puppet you are.

frustrated

Look straight at the audience. Imagine bugged-out eyes—as in, "Can you believe this?" Silently invite the audience into the puppet's exasperation.

hurt

With or without arm rods, just let that chin drop down, down, down, until, with a little hiccup, your puppet gives in to shoulder-shaking, melodramatic sobbing.

sleepy

Lullaby and goodnight . . . oh, so, so sleepy. "I think I'm just going to drop off to sleep right here. Nope. There. On second thought, maybe here." And with a heave and a sigh, snooooore.

Or do the boring lecture nod-and-snort. Drifting down, your head sinks slowly, slowly, and you're just starting to snore, when— SNORT! Your puppet's head jerks back up. "I'm awake. I'm awake."

embarrassed

Look down, maybe off to the side, whatever you need to do to avoid looking someone, anyone, in the eye. Glance back slowly at the audience and follow with a sad little shake of the head and a glance away.

shy

Tuck your head into your shoulder, sneak a peek out, and wait for it, wait . . . it won't be long before even the shyest of puppet folk will get bitten by the curiosity bug and have to look out at the audience. See, that wasn't so bad. None of us bite. Hard, anyway.

obnoxious

Overbearing, bossy, and no fun to be around, this character is forever in your face. "Whatcha doin'? Can I help? I'm better at doing that thingy than you are. Besides, I'm the boss; I get the final say. Ha!" Chin up, nose to the air, invade space, and crowd in. I'm sure you can manage it, if you just put your mind to it.

bold

Be confident, suave, and sassy. More than a bit bold, you're even a bit brassy. Stride with confidence, chest up and out. That's the ticket. It's the bold bird that gets the worm. Or was it the early worm that gets the bird?

stubborn

Stick your chin in the air and maybe accentuate it with a huff and a flip of the hair. Deliberate avoidance of eye contact with either the audience or the other puppets on the stage will lend an air of disregard. Cross those arms if you've got them, and set that mouth in a firm and unmovable line of disapproval.

Do keep an eye cocked toward the audience. They will lose interest if they cannot see the puppet's face for very long. That little tilt of the eye, all while studiously looking off into the distance, will allow the audience to stay connected to the puppet and to what the puppet is trying to express.

sneaky

Tippy toe with a little up and down movement, slowly and stealthily. If you've got hands, a little "shhhh" is a nice addition. Now put those skills to use. You see that reader over there? Shhhh . . . boo!

flirty

Look and avoid, then give a little giggle. Or motion forward in a come-hither or even a "Psst. Psst, I've got a secret" manner. Aim your attention at an audience member or an onstage puppet. This one is bound to get a great reaction.

thoughtful

Stop and look directly at an audience member. Shift a little, give a slight nod, and look at another person. This gives the impression of thoughtful consideration. Make your audience believe the puppet is thinking things through, or maybe let them wonder what exactly this puppet is considering. It can funny or serious; it just depends on what you have been doing before.

ANIMAL ATTITUDE

If your puppet is a realistic animal—not an anthropomorphized one, with human traits—your body movement will be different. Animal eye contact is very different from human—er, puppet eye contact. The shy koala will snuffle, tremble, and hide its face, while the bold cougar might just stare you down, eyeing you in a righteous state of hunger. Remember: keep that nose pointed at the audience.

animal movements

Glide, slide, sneak, and prowl; hunch your shoulders up, readying for a pounce! Or hop, skip, and flop like a bunny. Now is a good time to watch those animal nature shows, practice the movements yourself and get a real feel for it. Your animal puppet will thank you for your attention to detail. So will your audience.

Practicing without a stage? Give your animal a good base. Let it rest on your arm or cuddle up in the crook of your elbow. Go belly up and snuggly, or hold it close to your body to give it support.

When dealing with timid animals—whether they crawl out of a cupped hand or a pocket, burrow under your arm, or cling to your neck—these shy creatures will take a bit of coaxing. Give them some space and a friendly face until curiosity bites and they peek out at last. They'll eventually allow themselves to be drawn out for sharing time.

Yawn and rub the eyes; stretch and arch the back. All these movements go a long way toward showing a realistic, non-flop-me-every-which-way animal puppet.

Oh, and don't forget a well-timed sniff or two. Animal emotion can be just as powerful as human feelings.

the animal leap

Lean forward and bend your arms back slowly. You are the tiger, you are crouching, and you are almost ready to spring . . . now push off with a forward movement to indicate momentum. Jump up and move forward until you land, let the legs bend with the body slightly forward, then take a step or two and stop.

practice

Got your puppet ready to go? Good.

Now, assume he is an alien to the planet Earth and has just discovered a ball of yarn. He goes up to it, sniffs it, and looks at it. He looks back up at you, his human friend, for reassurance; he—sort of—trusts you. Give a nod of encouragement. With a little nudge . . . it rolls! Yikes! He retreats and burrows into your arms. But curiosity and the cat—well, a puppet is a lot like a cat. Your puppet inches back out; he takes another cautious look over, nudges it again, and is delighted to find that it rolls—again! Now it's all fun and games, but . . . you know what happens to a ball of yarn: it unravels. All too soon, you have a hog-tied and tangled alien on your hands. Eyeing you with remorse and a little bit of pleading, your puppet looks down at the yarn that is tangled all around, struggles a bit, and then turns back to you with a "please help me" look. Now you can scold your puppet for getting out of hand with a warning to not do that again . . . but, well . . . temptation is just too much, and just as you turn your attention away—pounce!

chapter 6

VOCAL LESSONS

GOOD GRACIOUS.

FINDING YOUR VOICE

Before you talk, remember that it's always polite to also do a fair amount of listening. Remember the two-ears-to-one-mouth ratio? Okay, I know that's not necessarily true in the puppet world, but it's still good advice.

"FLIPPING YOUR LID"

AND YET ANOTHER HINT FROM HIGGINS: LOOK LIKE YOU'RE LISTENING

Remember, a slight drop of the jaw shows a listening attitude. This also gives the puppet a pleasant "I'm almost smiling" appearance. Similarly, a tightly shut mouth is an indication of displeasure.

MASTERING MOUTH MANIPULATION

Listen and learn how to avoid "flipping your lid." No, I'm not talking attitude but about proper hand positioning for your puppet. If you talk with your nose aimed at the sky, consider the message you are sending: "I am not going to look at you, because I'm really worried about that spider above your head." And really, no one wants to be looking up someone else's nose.

Find your puppet's line of sight, angle your fingers so that your puppet is eyeing the audience, and then allow your thumb to do 70–80 percent of the work. Fingers should have no more than a 20 percent range of movement.

Let's get that mouth moving now. Do you remember grade school and how to clap out syllables? It's back to school and to clapping out individual syllables for your puppet.

Clap out the following: One, two, three, four, five, six, seven, eight, nine, ten.

How many claps did you get? If you got eleven claps (two claps for seven), give yourself a pat on the back.

Now reverse your clap. Instead of clapping your hands shut, open your hands for each syllable.

Correct puppet speak requires an open mouth for the vowels and a closed mouth for the consonants. Imagine you are spitting the words out, not biting down on them. When a puppet talks, the majority of the movement should be in the lower jaw. Drop the thumb down with each syllable. Thrust your fingers forward at the same time.

Ready to move on to full sentences? Practice following a conversation as it appears on the television. Or try your hand at a boring lecture . . . although you may want to hide those dexterous digits if you don't want to be thrown out for mocking the speaker.

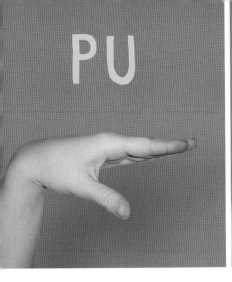
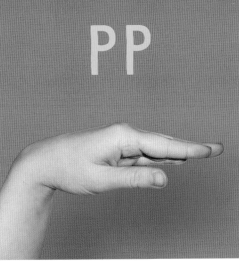
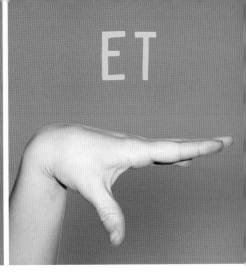

For longer phrases, open the mouth at the beginning of each sentence and end each sentence with a closed mouth. The middle can get muddled as long as you remember that it's the beginnings and the endings that are important—particularly if you have a long sentence, one in which it is easy to lose the flow or get lost in the phrase.

Remember, a little bit does it. A fully opened mouth not only indicates shouting, it's also just plain rude. Think of your everyday speech patterns. You don't open your mouth wide for each and every word. Save that view of the uvula for a wide-mouthed yawn. Just as any self-respecting author will judiciously restrict their use of the powerful shout of an exclamation point, a puppeteer should only use a fully opened mouth for the more extreme forms of expression.

Subtlety is key; savor the nuances of accurate mouth manipulation. With masterful head tilts and practiced body movements, you will soon find yourself the maestro in a symphony of puppet harmony.

MOVE THAT THUMB!

Place your hand under a table or desk. With the backs of your fingers pressing up against the bottom of the desk, practice moving your thumb down to do the talking. Remember: speak in open syll-a-bles.

FINDING CHARACTER VOICE

WATCH FUN EXAMPLES IN "MY FAIR PUPPET" VIDEO #5

If the voice fits, use it.

Speaking for your puppet should be like music to your ears. Literally. It should be like music, with highs and lows and everything in between. Just as if you were singing a song, your voice should have peaks and valleys. Practice your pitch. Experiment with your vocal range. How low can you go? How high can you fly? Each voice should have different timbres and dynamics. Listen to yourself, record it, and play it back. Can you sound like a child? An out-of-breath runner?

Sometimes it only takes a glance at your puppets to hear their voice; other times, you need to have an old fashioned one-on-one conversation with them. You've got to listen in order to hear what they want to sound like. Don't ever doubt the power of the unexpected. Perhaps your princess fairy has a voice like a trucker, and your trucker squawks like a parrot being stepped on. But then, that's just part of the fun of creation.

IDEAS FOR PRACTICE

Watching animated cartoons is a great way to experiment with voices. Tell everyone it's an assignment!

High, low, faster, slower, louder, softer. Try talking while placing your tongue on the roof of your mouth, or try behind your bottom teeth, front teeth, and so on.

Hold a two-handed conversation with yourself. Can you keep the voices straight? Do the voices sound distinctly different from each other?

Making your puppet's voice different from your own might take some practice. On your mark, get set, go!

- Nasal: all the sound comes from the nose
- Stuffy: all the sound goes through the mouth
- Breathy: run a lot of extra air through your words
- Gravelly: the voice resides deep in your throat
- Clear: a normal voice
- Articulate: each and every syllable spoken with precision and clarity
- Slurred: sleepy sounding or just studied and slow

conversations for starters

It takes two to tango . . . or carry on a conversation. When one puppet is talking alone, it's easy to tell who's doing the talking. If you have two or more puppets on scene, the audience can tell which one is talking by your use of different voices and also by who's doin' the movin'. If the voices sound the same, you need to use movement to distinguish who's talking when.

To take it even further, you can test out dialects and impersonations. The key is listening closely and repeating. Or you can check out an elocution book from your local library.

DICTION DILEMMAS: TRANSLATING PUPPET SPEAK

MISSING DICTION: When two or more puppets are speaking but only one puppet is present.

THE FIX: If this is a problem, form a puppet troupe; add puppeteers and puppets to fill in the holes. If you are flying solo, determine who gets to be on stage and who is more of a backstage presence.

RHYTHMIC DICTION: When working with a song recording and the words or lyrics are spoken too fast for a puppet to realistically pronounce each syllable.

THE FIX: The puppeteer should not try to hit every syllable. Instead, attempt to go with the flow and "feel" the rhythm instead. Also, know your material inside and out, upside and down, and backward and forward. If you can pull off a good rhythmic facsimile of the song, allowing the puppet to really get into the dance or body movements, no one will notice too much if the mouthworks are not 100 percent in line with the syllables.

POLYSYLLABIC DICTION: When a puppet's voice is speaking too fast for the puppeteer's hand to keep up.

THE FIX: As with any rule, knowing when to break it is half the battle. Remember: a rule is not substitute for a brain, and while you don't want to be skipping syllables unknowingly, it is perfectly okay to skip minor syllables deliberately for effect. If, as a puppetter, you focus on capturing the beginning and ending of each sentence, and it's a deliberate choice, this type of mouth movement versus actual speech can even be used as a device to create a breathless or faster paced and frightening chase scene.

PHONETIC DICTION: In an attempt to imitate real speech, the puppet's mouth mimics the movements of a real person's mouth. As an example, when saying "toad," the puppet will start with a closed mouth on the "t" sound, open for the "oa," close on the "d," and then slightly open the mouth again at the end. On the other hand, when speaking a long or loud "o," the puppet will open the mouth wider and wider until the end of the sound, when it will shut the sound off by closing the mouth shut.

THE FIX: Phonetic diction isn't necessarily a problem, but it can be extremely difficult to pull off. It is best suited to solo performers when speaking clearly, precisely, and slowly. Beginning puppeteers should focus on mastering syllabic diction first, i.e., the opening of the hand on the vowels and closing on the consonants.

THE BEST OPTION—SYLLABIC DICTION: When the mouth (hand) is open on the vowels and closed on the consonants.

ANOTHER EDICT FROM PROFESSOR SMARTY-PANTS-KNOW-IT-ALL HIGGINS:

Novice puppeteers frequently slip into a backwards syllabic diction rhythm (i.e., biting the vowels and spitting out the consonants). Practice is the cure.

throwing your voice

With practice and a few tips, you can gain mastery of the distant voice. The key is misdirection: turn your gaze upon the object you want your audience to believe is talking and act as if you heard it too. Can you see how timing and coordination are crucial? Practice will eventually make perfect—or so they tell me. I'm still waiting on the end result myself.

practice

Getting your multiple personalities in order is essential to any puppeteer working with more than one character. Test your skills by switching between three, four, or even ten personalities until you can do them in your sleep. Actually, by that time, you will be doing them in your sleep.

THE **RAAAAIN** IN SPAIN STAYS MAINLY IN THE PLAIN

POOR PUPPET

As always, practice makes perfect, but beware of puppet delirium.

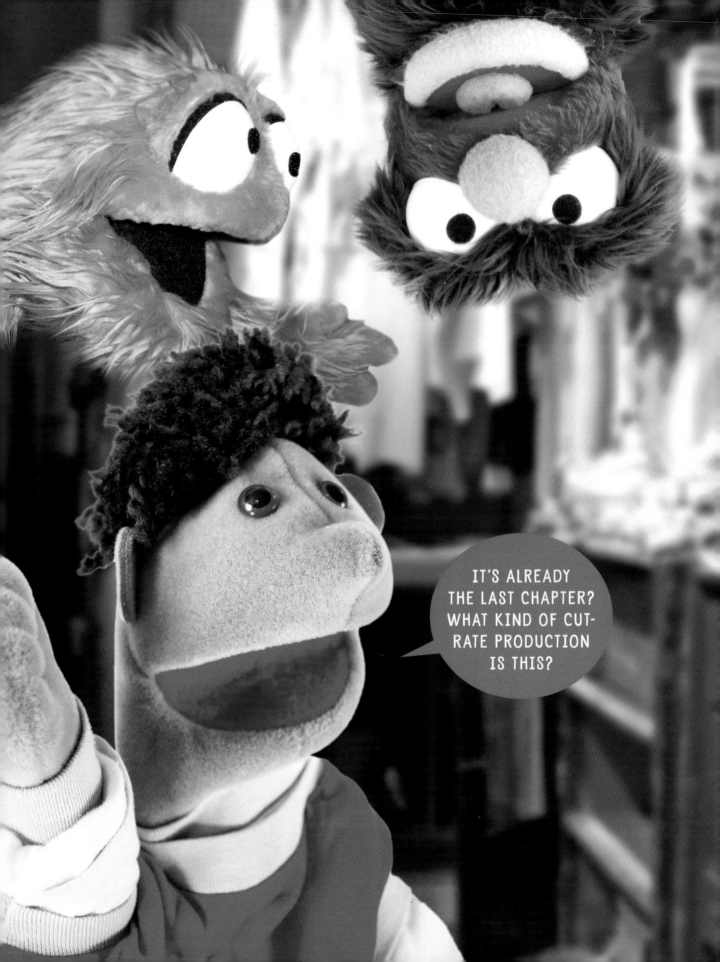

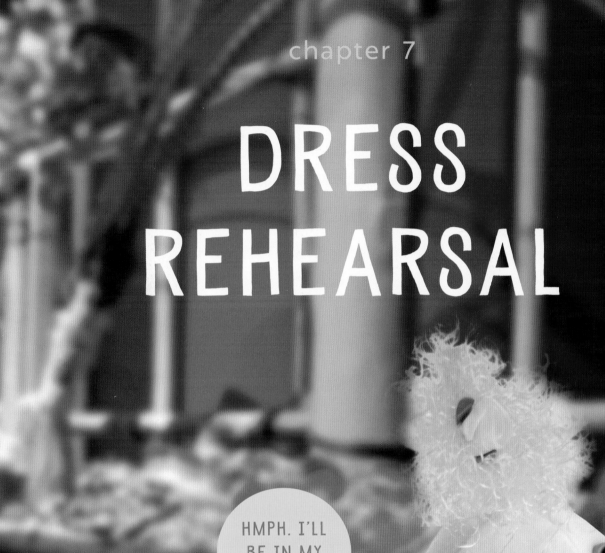

chapter 7

DRESS REHEARSAL

HMPH. I'LL BE IN MY *TRAILER!*

TAKE IT TO THE PEOPLE

La, la, la, la, la! This would be a lot more fun with some friends, so let's go gather them. Got everyone? Now we have what is called an audience (preferably not a captive one).

PERFORMING WITHOUT A STAGE

Performing without a stage means that you, the puppeteer, will be part of the show. You will have lines—maybe even a character—and the audience will see you. Ventriloquism is not required, but there are some basic ins and outs of putting on a puppet show without a stage.

First, you should have a focal point. The audience will look at whatever and wherever you look. You can instantly direct the audience's attention to the puppet by focusing your attention on the puppet. If the puppet is talking to the audience, the puppet needs to look at the audience. A puppet's gaze should only be directed at the puppeteer if the puppet and puppeteer are holding a brief discussion or conversation.

When working with two puppets, it is even more important to make sure your gaze is aimed at the puppet that is doing the talking. Yes, sometimes it's a bit of a tennis match, and if you mix up the voices—well, it's highly recommended that you have some good comebacks if, or when, it happens.

WHAT HAPPENED, PAIGE?

I DON'T KNOW. MUST BE A FROG IN MY THROAT; IT GOT REALLY DEEP THERE FOR A SECOND.

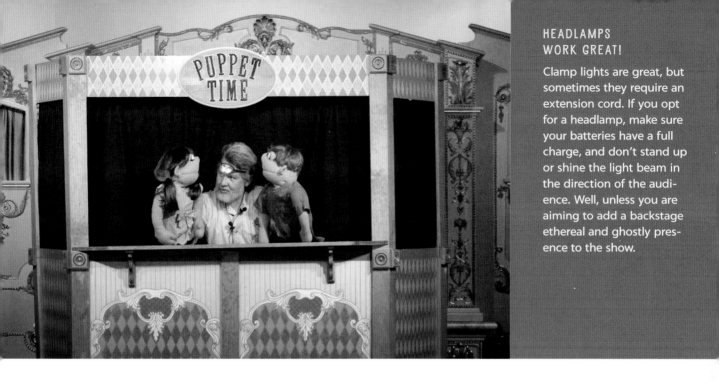

HEADLAMPS WORK GREAT!

Clamp lights are great, but sometimes they require an extension cord. If you opt for a headlamp, make sure your batteries have a full charge, and don't stand up or shine the light beam in the direction of the audience. Well, unless you are aiming to add a backstage ethereal and ghostly presence to the show.

If you believe the puppet is real, so will your audience. They will be drawn in, and before long, they will be make-believing right along with you.

This is not to say that you can't look elsewhere. The key to excellence in puppeteering is knowing the rules so that you know when and how to break them if necessary.

PERFORMING WITH A STAGE

Anything can become your stage. You just need something to hide behind, and *viola!* You can begin.

entrances and exits

Remember our movement exercises? Let's start practicing them again, this time with the benefit of a stage.

- Bounce with forward movement to walk.
- Can you take the stairs? Try two at a time, then three. Now slide down! Wheeee!
- Pop up in a surprise attack! Channel a Jack-in-the-box. Is Jack still in the box?
- Have a chase scene. Utilize the space above the stage, to the side, in the middle. Audiences appreciate exhilarating and surprising chase scenes. Jack is now definitely out of the box.

how to set up behind the stage

Whether you're all alone or working in a very close team, a smoothly run show is the sign of an organized work area. Tape up your script and bring a headlamp or battery-operated touch light in case of darkness. If possible, place your puppets upside down on hooks for easier, one-handed access. These tips will make your show run smoothly and problem-free—well, as problem-free as any live performance can be.

WATCH FUN EXAMPLES
IN "MY FAIR PUPPET"
VIDEO #4

PERFORMANCE PITFALLS

Be careful to avoid these problems when performing with puppets onstage.

deadly quicksand syndrome

It's not easy to keep your arms and elbows at a 90-degree angle while only moving your wrists and hands. Because of this, puppets have the tendency to slowly sink way down south. Watch out for the sinking pothole performances wherein nothing but a tuft of hair is visible to the audience.

TIP: DO YOUR EXERCISES

Want to avoid the dreaded fatigued-to-death arm? Do your exercises faithfully. Pump those pecs, power up those upper arms, and flex those fingers. Exercise is good for the body and good for the puppet . . . show.

the puppet whisperer

While this might work well with horses, dogs, and babies, a puppet whisperer is sudden death to puppets. Make sure your voice is loud and clear. Nothing ruins a show more than having a room full of "What did he say?" Or just a chorus of "What???"

Always be aware of your audience. If your show is the funniest thing you've ever performed but you get no response, it might be due to the fact that they can't hear you. And while it is a fine line between a yell and a shout, when in doubt, pump up the volume (unless you're microphoned—then that "What did he say?" might be due to the ringing in the audience's ears).

Even if the puppet is "whispering," the words should be audible and exaggerated. The audience will get the idea.

the rip van winkle

Keep your puppet alive and active. Don't fall asleep on stage; it could prove contagious and your audience might decide to nod off too. Sometimes the pressure of always being "on" can be too much for your puppet and, unknowingly, they slump or rest on stage. You might not even be aware you're doing this, but your audience will notice the naptime and wonder if that's part of the show. Keep your puppet alive and moving. Even a brief shake of the head will convince them that you're still performing.

unintended arm exposure

You need to be in the habit of keeping your hands up, but like any tasteful show, you never want to show skin. Make sure you're covered from where the puppet ends to where your armpit begins. Remember: the sky's the limit, so reach for the stars; just don't let the audience see any naked and hairy armpits—er, I mean, arm bits—while you're doing it.

SPITTING IMAGE.

WAIT A SECOND, ARE THOSE SUPPOSED TO BE *ME*?

the headless chicken effect

A common problem with newly minted puppeteers is the tendency to move unnecessarily. Don't act like a chicken with its head cut off. While it is important to have almost constant movement, make sure it is necessary movement. No needless flopping or flapping allowed.

UNEXPECTED CELL PHONE RING?

Pause the action and allow the puppet to comment on the interruption. "And now we pause today's performance for a cell phone break as we listen to the ringing tones of [you can insert the name of the ringtone if you know it] . . . "

unintended curtain movement

Curtain movement, whether it's from an audience escapee or a puppeteer's goof—while not a frequent occurrence—is an occasional problem. A good sense of humor and the ability to recover gracefully along with some quick-witted quips are about the only defenses you have to this issue. You can always take a page from Punch and Judy and enlist the services of a Bottler to contain your crowd and keep them in their proper place.

backstage sounds

While there is not a whole lot you can do to avoid an accident, it does take a certain amount of poise and humor to recover gracefully, if not humorously, from a larger-than-life gaffe. Prepare ahead of time by practicing a wisecracking comeback or two. And never forget that when "life" happens, it's a good policy to never take things too seriously; enjoy the moment, and if you're going to laugh about it eventually, it's best to get started on the laughter sooner rather than later.

mischievous children

Puppets are miracle workers! Hard-to-instruct children will often find themselves following the directions of a dictatorial puppet over the well-meaning threats of a frustrated parent or caregiver. Keep the voice going: "We interrupt our usual programming for young Susie Q. Headstrong, a curious little . . ." Who knows? It might prove to be such a hit that you plan it next time.

BUT THEY GOT MY NOSE ALL WRONG!

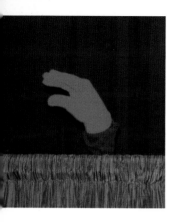

unforeseen incidents

Enter the stage hand! A simple glove—one you already have on your hand as part of your black sleeve—could quickly and easily come on stage to do a little fixing, put hats back on, and do some miscellaneous rearranging. Craft some snazzy dialogue to go along with it and you've turned an unfortunate incident into a fun-filled, are-you-sure-you-didn't-plan-that folly.

mistaken voice

Otherwise called the "accidental teenage boy tenor" or the "gravel-throated maiden mistake." If you work long enough with puppets, this will happen to you. Prepare in advance by practicing, practicing, and practicing some more. Practice not only the script as written, but also those comebacks and jokes for recovering from the accidental voice mistake.

A NOTE ON SCRIPTS

Need a little help with your story? You can use many different sources for your actual script or for script inspiration. Remember to not use copyrighted material without asking for the author's permission, and always give the author credit for their work.

suggested sources of inspiration

- *Play* magazine
- *Cricket* magazine
- Picture books
- Beginning reader books
- Scour the folk and fairy tale bookshelves for tales familiar and not-so-familiar

The best advice is to have fun. Use the resource books and tales, then adjust and rewrite them to fit your audience's age level. Have a great one-liner or punch line? Create a story that takes the audience on a rollicking ride that ends on that one-liner.

Play with word phrases or twisted and mixed-up words. Create a story that takes advantage of those misconstrued words. Play off a puppet's natural naiveté, and even use their unique shortcomings. If a puppet can't read or mixes up their words—much like a young elementary-aged audience—then create a storyline where those beginning reader mistakes happen, with the resulting hilarious consequences.

Puppeteers frequently find themselves looking at the world from a different perspective than others; embrace your unique and individual take on the world. Remember what it was like as a young child; recall your own trials, mistakes, and "learning" opportunities. The world is a stage, or so they say, so by golly use it and all its lessons on your personal puppet stage.

RESOURCES

REFERENCE, HOW-TO, AND DEFINITIONS

WORKING WITH FABRIC AND FURS

A little knowledge goes a long way, and going with or against the grain, stretch, or nap of a fabric can make a big difference in your finished product.

A FEW BASICS:

SELVAGE

Selvage is the machined edge, or self-finished edge, of fabric that keeps the fabric from unraveling or fraying. Many manufacturers will include printed fabric details and websites along the selvage that are particularly helpful when you fall in love with and would like more of the fabric.

GRAIN

The grain of the fabric is the direction in which the threads run. If you cut up from the selvage, following the grain of the fabric at a 90-degree angle, you will find that many fabrics can be torn instead of cut. Quick and easy, it's a great way to square off a portion of the fabric. Caution: not all fabrics will tear.

BIAS

The bias of a fabric runs at a 45-degree angle from the selvage. It runs crosswise in an X shape. This is where most of the stretch in any fabric comes from.

NAP

The nap of a fabric—the texture—refers to a raised or visible fabric direction. Not all fabrics will have a visible nap. When using furs, the nap is the direction in which the hairs lay. Furs are easy. What's frustrating is when you either accidentally cut the pattern out upside down or when you don't notice the direction of a fine velvet-length nap until the project is sewn and done.

CUTTING FUR

First, if you are getting fur from a brick-and-mortar location and you have the ability to be at the cutting table, have the employee test the fabric to see if it can be ripped instead of cut. Ripping a straight line is a sure way to avoid messy cut fur edges, and the rip will

always be square to the selvage edge—a definite plus when you work with the nap later. When ripping on your own, make a small cut through the selvage edge of the fabric. Then grab either side of the cut and rip away. Stop at the next selvage edge, and cut with scissors at that point.

When you are cutting furs, particularly the long and luxurious kind, we strongly suggest you don't go in chopping with the scissors in a willy-nilly fashion. Instead, choose a very sharp pair of scissors, and with a lot of care, slip the cutting edge of the scissors along the base of the fur strands and only snip the mesh fabric, avoiding all fur. When done correctly, the result is a mess-free cutting zone and intact furry strands that make sewing a seemingly seamless puppet easier.

TRACING HELPS

Want to make fur cutting easier? Trace the pattern with a permanent marker, remove the pattern, and then cut the fur.

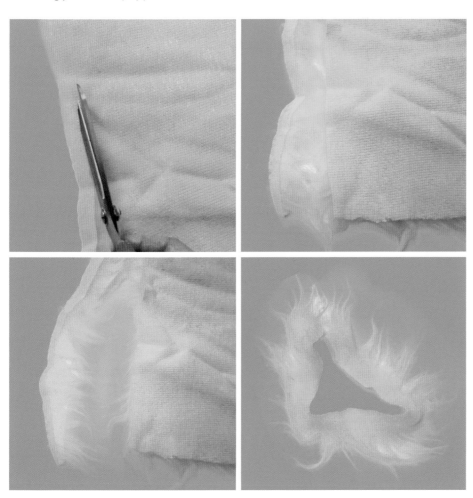

SEWING FUR

Sewing fur by hand is usually the best option for a seamless look. But if you know you want to use the sewing machine, the best way to hide your seams is to prevent as much of the fur from being sewn into the stitches as possible. The use of a small brush and some careful pinning go a long way toward making your puppet as seam-free as possible.

CUTTING FROM A PATTERN

When using a pattern with your fabric, remember:

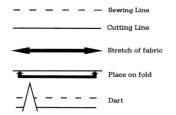

— — — — — — Sewing Line

———————— Cutting Line

◄——————► Stretch of fabric

Place on fold

Dart

- Seam lines are dotted lines.
- Cut lines are solid lines.
- A line with two arrows pointing to the same edge marks a fold line. Fold the fabric and pin pattern with the designated fold line on the fold.
- Darts are shown as the large triangles that cut into the fabric.
- All patterns in the book are designed to be placed on the wrong side of the fabric.

SEWING

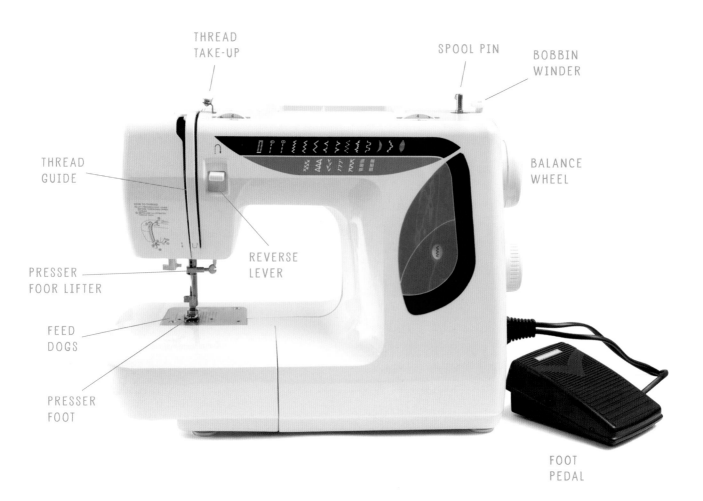

THREAD
TAKE-UP

SPOOL PIN

BOBBIN
WINDER

THREAD
GUIDE

BALANCE
WHEEL

REVERSE
LEVER

PRESSER
FOOR LIFTER

FEED
DOGS

PRESSER
FOOT

FOOT
PEDAL

SEWING BY MACHINE

Backstitch at the beginning and end of each seam to lock threads and prevent the seams from unraveling.

Most puppet fabrics have a bit of give to them—that is, they stretch. To prevent popped threads from an accidental overstretching of the puppet's seams, plan on stretching the fabric as you sew.

darts

A dart is a folded, cut-out wedge of fabric that, when sewn together, tailors a flat fabric into a form-fitting rounded shape.

small-rolled seams and hems

Small-rolled seams are ideal when you want a neat, finished edge. As a beginner, you might consider adding some sewing pins to hold the fabric in a small tucked roll. A pro can usually just tuck and roll as they go.

sewing corners

When sewing around a sharp corner, you can get the best look by sewing up to the edge, then:

1 Push the needle down.

2 Raise the presser foot up.

3 Turn fabric.

4 Put the presser foot back down.

5 Continue to sew in the new direction.

easing fabric

When working with stretchy fabrics, frequently one side will stretch a little bit more or less than the other. If left unchecked, you end up with a mismatch in length by the end of the seam. Or even worse, in a bad attempt to fix the problem, the seamstress/seamster ends up with tucks and folds in the most inopportune places.

A lot of this can be avoided with careful pinning. But if you notice that maybe the top fabric is stretching a bit long and the bottom is a smidge too short, before it gets out of hand, start stretching the bottom fabric as much as possible while gently pushing and easing the top fabric under the presser foot. Careful: don't push too hard, or you will end up with those tucks after all. Reverse directions as needed (i.e., longer bottom and shorter top fabric call for pushing and easing the bottom while stretching the top).

VEGETABLE OIL CLEANER

Gluing or using spray adhesive? Clean sticky fingers from an abundance of spray adhesive or contact cement with vegetable oil and a strong paper towel.

KEEP THE GLUE FROM STICKING

Hot glue a bit hot? Dip your fingers in water before pressing two sides of a hot-glued piece of fabric together. The glue is less likely to stick to your skin.

SEE IT IN ACTION IN "ADVANCED PUPPET WORKSHOP" VIDEO #4

SEWING BY HAND

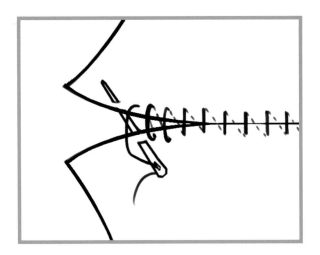

whipstitch

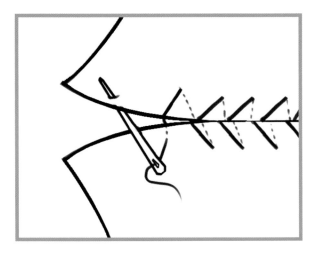

baseball stitch

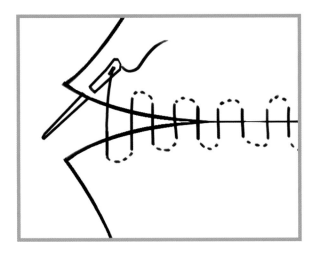

ladder stitch

reverse ladder stitch

Reversing the ladder stitch is also an option. Just reverse the hidden-inside segments with the showing-on-the-outside segments.

locking the ladder stitch

Lock the ladder stitch from possible unraveling by forming a knot every ten to twenty stitches. A knot is formed when you run a needle through the loop of a stitch just as you are pulling it closed. Then pull it tight. Don't knot with every stitch—you'll end up with a seam that has no give to it.

WELL *THIS* SHOULD LEAVE HIM IN STITCHES.

PUPPETEER'S EMERGENCY KIT

When traveling with puppets, it's a good idea to take a page out of the Boy Scout manual and be prepared. Having an emergency kit—not unlike having a set of jumper cables stowed in the car trunk or carrying a travel kit of bandages and medical supplies—is never a bad move.

Here are some things we suggest you pack in your puppeteer's emergency kit:

- Permanent marker, black
- Notepad
- Pen and pencil
- Needle with pre-threaded and knotted thread, in various colors from dark to light
- Embroidery needles
- Heavy-duty quilting thread
- Masking tape
- Electrical tape
- Duct tape
- Scissors
- Safety pins
- T-pins or long sewing pins

Traveling with a stage? Add these to your kit:

- Stool
- Rubber mallet
- Pliers
- Extra hardware or supplies for your specific stage

OPTIONAL:

- Hinged Gate-Fold Stage Supplies
- Extra wing nuts
- Extra nails for wing hinges

RESOURCES AND DEFINITIONS

While a lot of puppet making can be done with what you have on hand, there are times when you might want the real deal. The good stuff. The I-did-not-just-recycle-Mom's-old-coat-for-its-faux-fur. This section is for you.

Oh, and for anyone wanting additional resources and materials' definitions.

Due to the changing nature of the web and our wish to keep you as updated and informed as possible, we have opted to host a website that can change as often as needed. Join us for periodic tips, additional how-to and where-to links, puppet shows, community connections, and more.

Visit the *Dressing the Naked Hand* website at www.DressingTheNakedHand.com.

ONLINE RESOURCES

ATLAS FOAM PRODUCTS USA

www.atlasfoam.com

LAMPLIGHT FEATHER

www.tonyhill.net/ostrichfeathers.html

DISTINCTIVE FABRIC

www.distinctivefabric.com

OUT OF THE BOX PUPPETS

www.outoftheboxpuppets.com

MENDEL'S

www.mendels.com

SMOOTH-ON

www.smooth-on.com

WEIRD KID (FLAT RATE $25 SHIPPING)

www.weirdkidstore.com

PROJECT PUPPET

www.projectpuppet.com

A WORD ABOUT MATERIALS

The hardest part about finding supplies—at least in today's age of Internet searching—is knowing what to search for. The following terms will often be enough to get you where you are going:

ABS PLASTIC (acrylonitrile butadiene styrene): a hard shell plastic

ANTRON FLEECE: also known as "Muppet® fleece"

BATTING: also known as "wadding" in the UK

BOOKBINDER'S BOARD: also known as "cover board" or "binder's board"

CONTACT CEMENT: a neoprene-based adhesive

CORRUGATED PLASTIC: durable, waterproof, and lightweight plastic cardboard.

COVER BOARD (see "bookbinder's board")

CRAFT FOAM SHEETS: readily available sheets of thin, flexible, and porous foam

CURTAIN OR DRAPERY FABRIC: a heavier-weight home decor cloth

CUSHION FOAM (see "poly foam"): also known as "upholstery foam"

DOLL JOINTS: commercial two-part joints

DOOR HINGE: common household hinge used for doors

DRILL: electric or hand tool for drilling holes in wood

ELECTRIC CARVING KNIFE: commonly known as a "turkey knife"

EXPANDING FOAM (see "isocyanate and polyol resin"): also known as "spray foam insulation"

FABRIC DYE: liquid or powder

FELT: non-woven textile of matted and compressed fibers

FLEECE FABRIC: a soft fabric with a deep pile

FOAM CORE BOARD: laminated poster board with a polystyrene center

FUR FABRIC: often called "synthetic fur" or "faux fur"

GAUGE: refers to the size or the diameter (not the length) of a rod or stick

HACKSAW: a fine-toothed handsaw on a tension frame

HEAT GUN: emits a stream of high-temperature air

HEAT SHRINK TUBING (see "polyolefin"): nylon tubing that shrinks in only one direction

HIGH-TEMPERATURE HOT GLUE GUN: adhesive gun using glue sticks that melt under high heat

INTERFACING: Pellon® or another brand of stiff and non-fraying utility fabric that can be substituted for paper to make long-lasting patterns

ISOCYANATE AND POLYOL RESIN: also known as "expanding foam insulation" or "spray foam insulation"

LATEX RUBBER (see "polyvinyl acetate")

LIFT-OFF HINGE: also known as "slip joint hinge," "take-apart hinge," or "cabinet hinge"

MASONITE®: a pressure-molded hardboard made into sheets

OSTRICH FEATHERS: dyed and sold in bunches or strung together

PARTICLE BOARD: inexpensive composite board made into rigid sheets

PELLON® (see "interfacing"): a lightweight, usually stiff and non-fraying utility fabric

POLYETHYLENE PLASTIC: a common plastic such as the kind used for gallon ice cream buckets

POLY FOAM: cushion or upholstery foam

POLYOLEFIN TUBING: heat shrink tubing that shrinks in only one direction

POLYVINYL ACETATE: latex rubber

PVC PIPE: polyvinyl chloride pipe

RASP: a rough metal file used to shape wood; useful in shaping foam

ROTARY TOOL: a sander with sanding drum attachments

ROUND ROD (see "steel wire")

SAFETY DOLL EYES: commercial plastic eyes with a push-on washer for a secure hold

SHEETING WOOD: finely sanded sheets of wooden or veneer floor sheeting

SPRAY ADHESIVE: general-purpose to high-performance-hold adhesive glue

STEEL WIRE (round rod or welder's wire): varying gauges available; an alternative to wooden dowels

SUITING FABRIC: lightweight and semi-sheer rayon, nylon, or tropical weight fabrics

TRICOT FABRIC: a lightweight fabric that allows puppeteers to see their audience without being seen

UTILITY KNIFE: uses either a fixed blade, a folding blade, or disposable breakaway blades

VENTILATION MASK: also known as a "dust, mist, and fume respirator"

WOODEN DOWELS: unfinished rounded wood dowels in varying gauges and lengths

Most products can be found in hardware, fabric, craft, and hobby stores.
We highly recommend researching any online source before purchasing online.

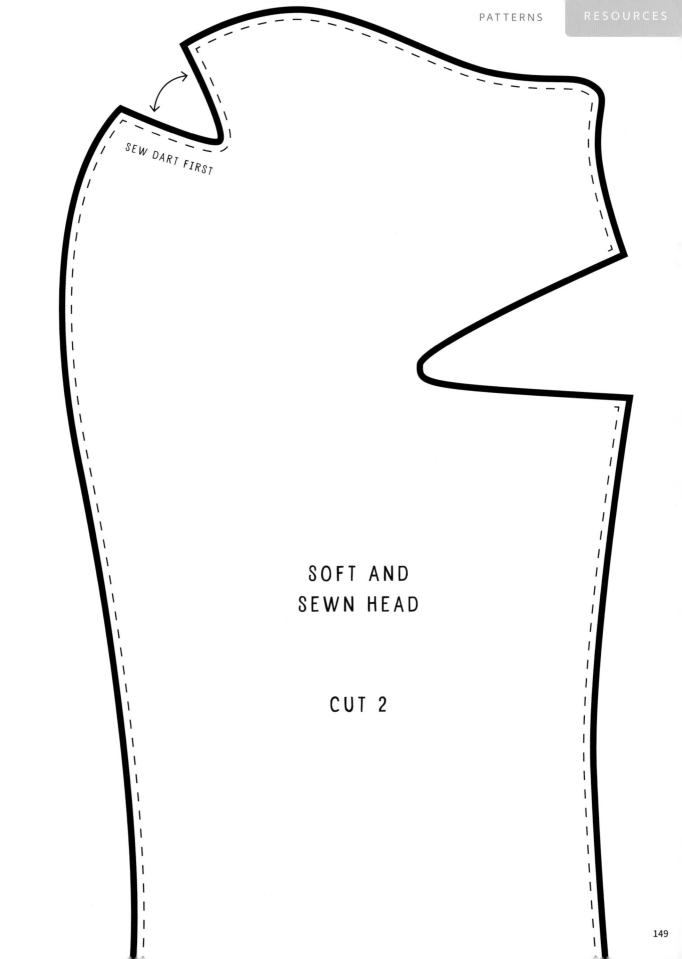

SEW DART FIRST

SOFT AND
SEWN HEAD

CUT 2

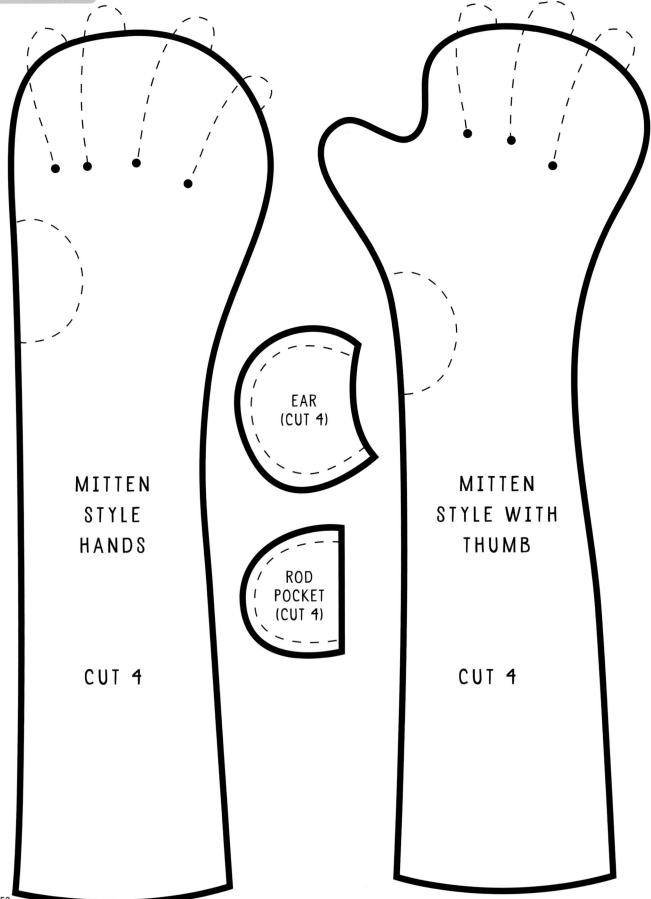

MITTEN
STYLE
HANDS

EAR
(CUT 4)

ROD
POCKET
(CUT 4)

MITTEN
STYLE WITH
THUMB

CUT 4

CUT 4

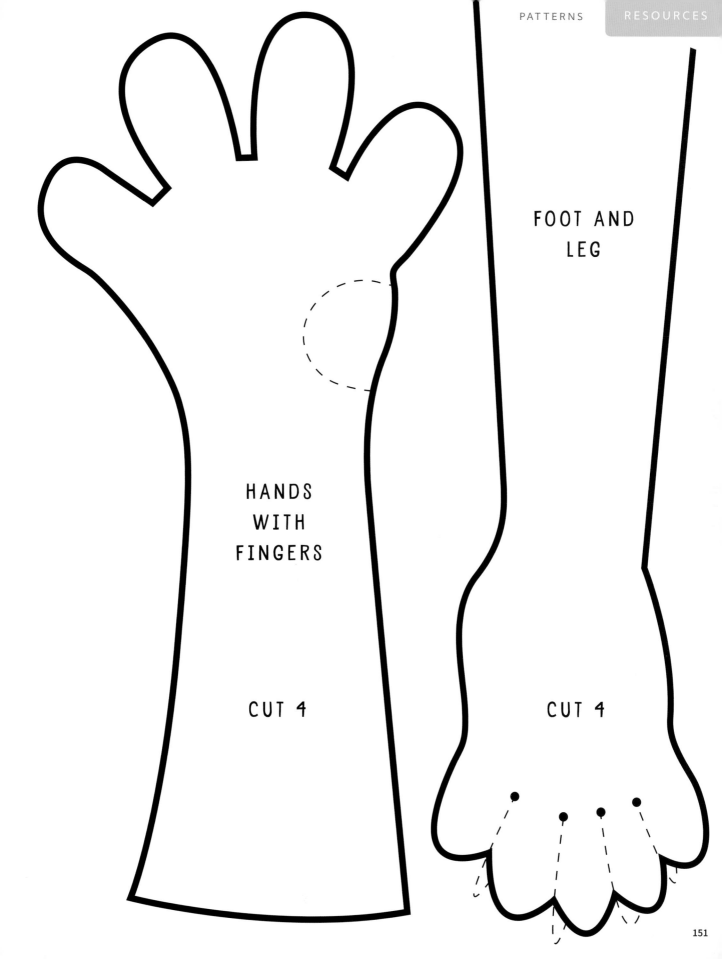

HANDS
WITH
FINGERS

CUT 4

FOOT AND
LEG

CUT 4

TORSO TUBE

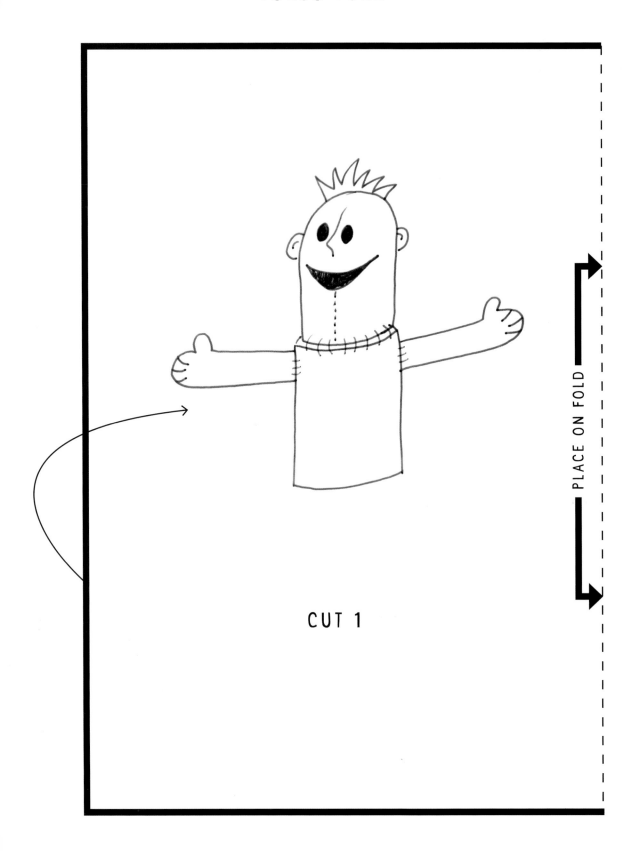

CUT 1

PLACE ON FOLD

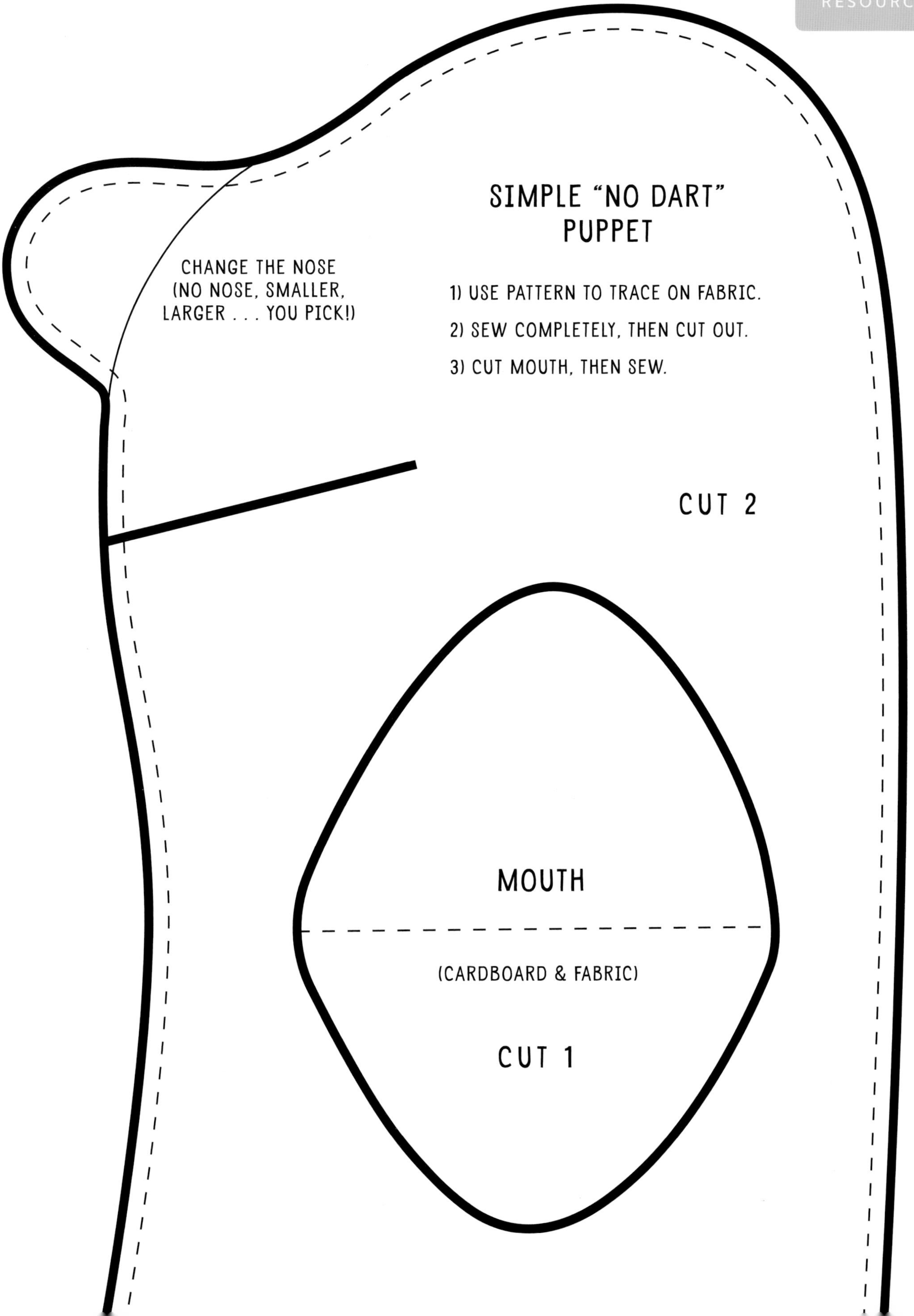

CHANGE THE NOSE
(NO NOSE, SMALLER,
LARGER . . . YOU PICK!)

SIMPLE "NO DART" PUPPET

1) USE PATTERN TO TRACE ON FABRIC.

2) SEW COMPLETELY, THEN CUT OUT.

3) CUT MOUTH, THEN SEW.

CUT 2

MOUTH

(CARDBOARD & FABRIC)

CUT 1

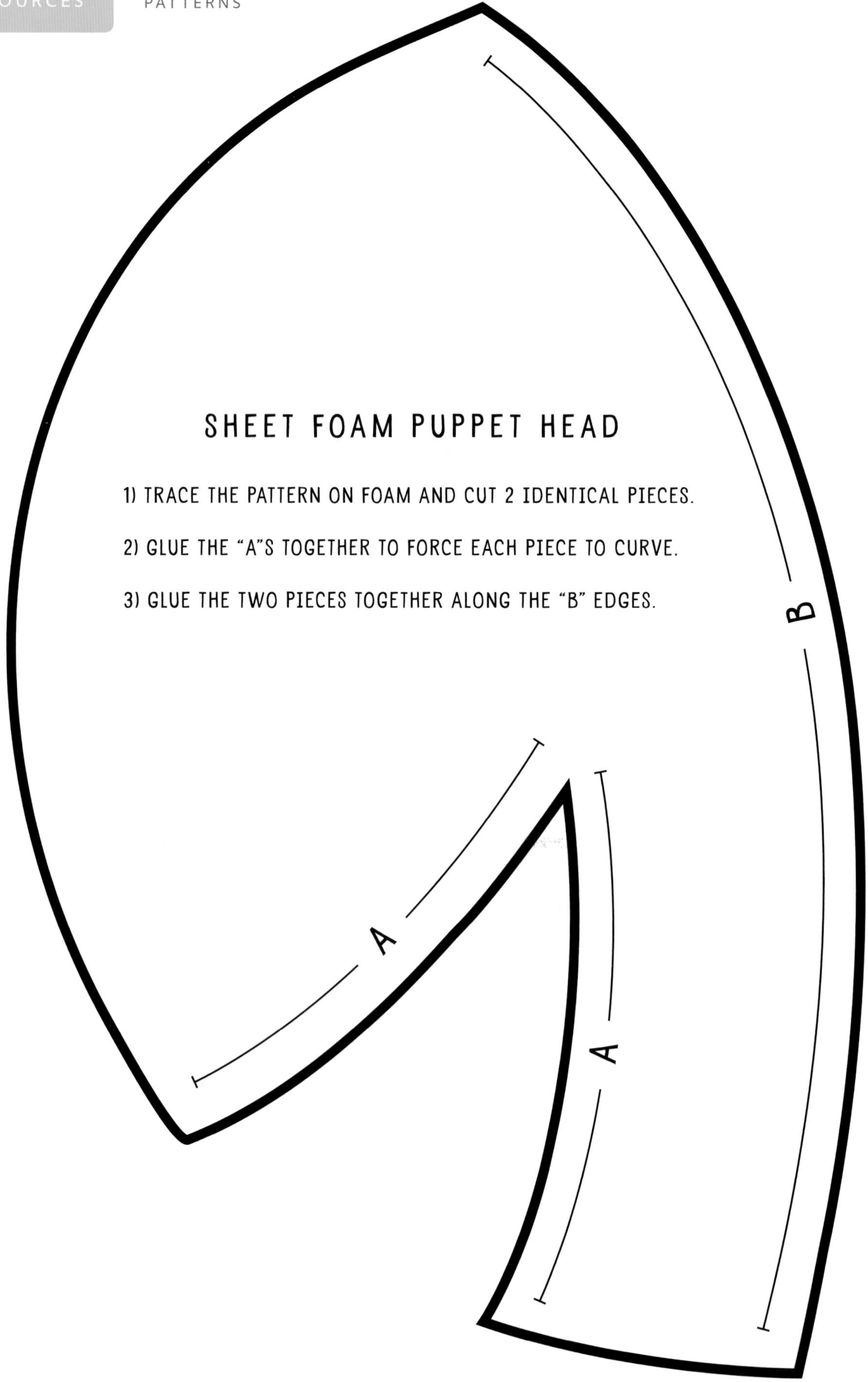

SHEET FOAM PUPPET HEAD

1) TRACE THE PATTERN ON FOAM AND CUT 2 IDENTICAL PIECES.

2) GLUE THE "A"S TOGETHER TO FORCE EACH PIECE TO CURVE.

3) GLUE THE TWO PIECES TOGETHER ALONG THE "B" EDGES.

B

A

A

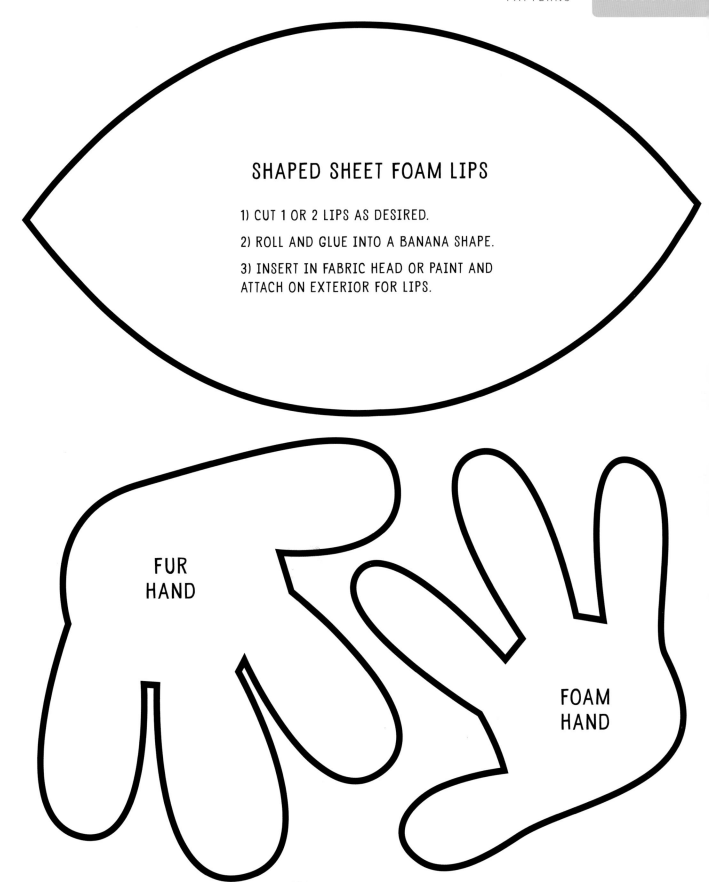

SHAPED SHEET FOAM LIPS

1) CUT 1 OR 2 LIPS AS DESIRED.

2) ROLL AND GLUE INTO A BANANA SHAPE.

3) INSERT IN FABRIC HEAD OR PAINT AND ATTACH ON EXTERIOR FOR LIPS.

FUR
HAND

FOAM
HAND

ADVANCED HARD MOUTHPALATE

(RESIZE AS NEEDED TO FIT THE HEAD OF YOUR PUPPET)

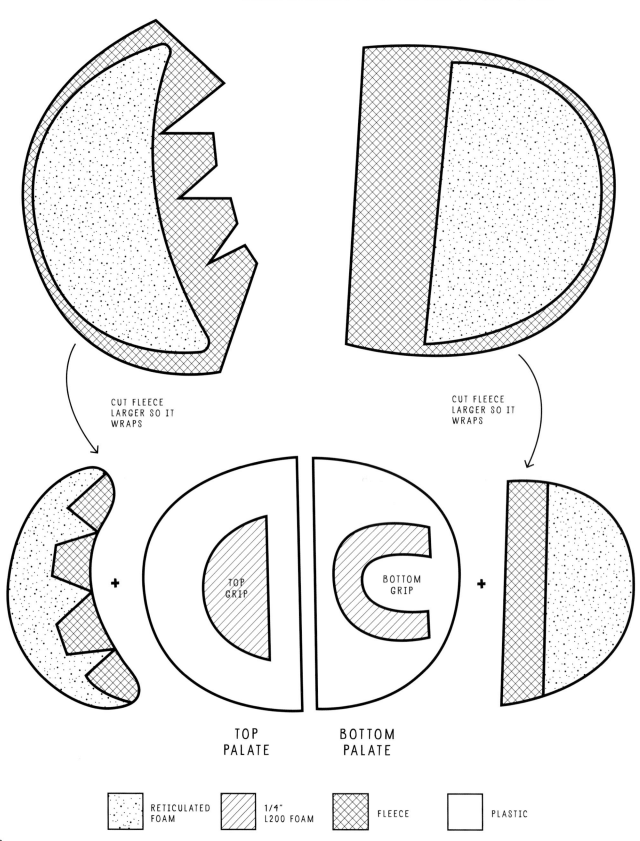

CUT FLEECE
LARGER SO IT
WRAPS

CUT FLEECE
LARGER SO IT
WRAPS

TOP
GRIP

BOTTOM
GRIP

TOP
PALATE

BOTTOM
PALATE

RETICULATED
FOAM

1/4"
L200 FOAM

FLEECE

PLASTIC

SPECIAL THANK YOU

It started with Mark Pulham—children's librarian, puppeteer extraordinaire, improvisation king, yearly summer reading program emcee—and his puppets. An all-around favorite, Mark is known not only for leaving scores of kids in fits of giggles, but also for his ability to have the adults in his audiences streaming tears of laughter—me included. This book is what I learned from him and a few other great puppet makers and performers who I corralled and talked into teaching me.

One of those others, Joe Flores, is one of the most persistent, non-stop, and over-the-top creative puppet makers I've had the opportunity to work with. Joe was instrumental in getting this book off the ground. It was Joe who insisted I write the book. It was Joe who checked in with me weekly—for years—always bringing new ideas, sketching out how-tos whenever I was stumped, and providing much-needed motivation.

During our journey to publication, we found Dallin Blankenship, yet another storytelling puppet maker, from the nearby Provo Public Library. When Dallin found that he was always missing characters for his stories, he decided to make them himself. Dallin soon found an internship and then a job at The Puppet School in Los Angeles. Now, he is back in Utah, busy pursuing his Puppet Master of the Universe Doctorate as a member of the Naked Hand team.

A special thank-you needs to go out to Paul Green for his many hours shooting and processing video. Also the talented hand of Jess Smart Smiley. Additionally, Susan Neidert with the World of Puppetry Museum for her great help in the history segment. Thanks to Carolyn Frank for her willingness to help. Thanks to Cindy Taylor and Kathy Adams for their amazing puppet skills and insight. I can't forget to thank the tremendous Utah writing community for the wealth of knowledge and opportunity, from the Writing and Illustrating for Young Readers Conference members to Rick Walton, picture book extraordinaire, and mentor of all mentors. And, of course, a big thank-you to the Orem Public Library, with our amazing library patrons and the best Children's Section staff ever. And one last big thank-you to the Timpanogos Storytelling Festival for allowing me to immerse myself in puppet heaven each year in the Fanfare tent.

None of this book would have gone further than a fevered dream if not for the vision of Familius's Christopher Robbins—yes, you know by his name he's one of us. Forever cheering me on, Christopher and the Familius family never lost faith. And more than that, they had my back. I can't express how grateful I am to the entire team—our editor, Brooke Jorden, for her tremendous commitment; our publicist, Kirsten Nicholas, for her enthusiasm—and all those who worked with me on the path to publication.

Another special, huge, tremendous, holy-cow-this-would-not-have-been-possible-without-you thank-you to David Miles, our brilliant book designer with his mad design skills and never-flagging enthusiasm for the book.

Last, but certainly not least, a heartfelt thank you to all my family: Jason, Justin, and Alexis—my three supportive and amazing kids—and to my dear husband, Brian, without whom there would have been many more dinner-less nights and mountains of laundry. Thank you for keeping the household on track and the yard looking like a million bucks.

It does take a village—or, in my case, the whole city and a publishing house, to boot—to succeed. Now it's your turn. Take the book for a spin. Enjoy the DVD. We dare you not to laugh. Visit the website at www. DressingTheNakedHand.com, and then drop us a line or two at DressingNakedHands@gmail.com. We'd love to hear from you.

—Amy White and the *Naked Hand* team

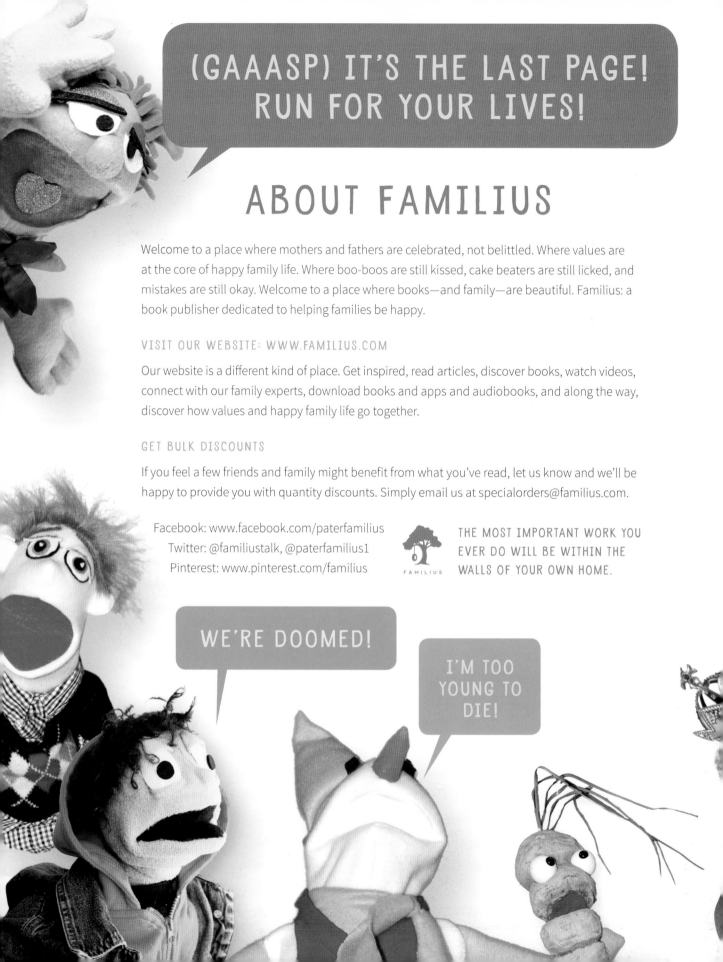

(GAAASP) IT'S THE LAST PAGE! RUN FOR YOUR LIVES!

ABOUT FAMILIUS

Welcome to a place where mothers and fathers are celebrated, not belittled. Where values are at the core of happy family life. Where boo-boos are still kissed, cake beaters are still licked, and mistakes are still okay. Welcome to a place where books—and family—are beautiful. Familius: a book publisher dedicated to helping families be happy.

VISIT OUR WEBSITE: WWW.FAMILIUS.COM

Our website is a different kind of place. Get inspired, read articles, discover books, watch videos, connect with our family experts, download books and apps and audiobooks, and along the way, discover how values and happy family life go together.

GET BULK DISCOUNTS

If you feel a few friends and family might benefit from what you've read, let us know and we'll be happy to provide you with quantity discounts. Simply email us at specialorders@familius.com.

Facebook: www.facebook.com/paterfamilius
Twitter: @familiustalk, @paterfamilius1
Pinterest: www.pinterest.com/familius

FAMILIUS

THE MOST IMPORTANT WORK YOU EVER DO WILL BE WITHIN THE WALLS OF YOUR OWN HOME.

WE'RE DOOMED!

I'M TOO YOUNG TO DIE!

ABOUT THE AUTHORS

AMY WHITE

Amy is a children's literature specialist at the Orem Public Library and a puppeteer. A dedicated Laptime and Storytime enthusiast and blogger, Amy uses puppets on an almost daily basis. Amy is an advocate for early literacy and believes that puppets are a great avenue for sparking an early interest in story. A longtime advocate of storytelling and puppetry, Amy has been an integral part of bringing puppets to the annual Timpanogos Storytelling Festival since 1997. As addicts to all things puppet, Amy and Mark teach puppetry at the Orem Library's Storyteller Training Workshops on Wannabe Puppetry, along with other local and state puppeteer training series.

MARK PULHAM

Mark Pulham, Utah Arts Educator of the Year 2006, is a teacher, librarian, puppeteer, and actor who currently works for the Orem Public Library. As a teacher, Mark often used his puppets to teach the lessons, literally. When his classroom didn't have an aide, he produced one from the closet—a puppet student teacher who could scold and tell the kids what to do—one the kids really listened to. Mark frequently teaches puppet-making workshops and performs puppet shows at schools, libraries, and centers for the arts.

DALLIN BLANKENSHIP

When Dallin Blankenship, an Alabama native and computer animation expert, took a job at the Provo Library as a storytime specialist, he found that the stories he wanted to share were frequently missing one or more puppet characters. Not one to give up so easily, Dallin began to make the characters himself. Soon the talented puppeteer found an internship and then a job at The Puppet School in Los Angeles. Now, while he is back in Utah showing off his talents in the art of animation at Brigham Young University, Dallin is also busy pursuing his Puppet Master of the Universe Doctorate as a member of the *Naked Hand* team.

THE END

Aaahhhh......